THE BIBLE DOCTRINE
OF ATONEMENT

THE BIBLE DOCTRINE
OF ATONEMENT

SIX LECTURES GIVEN IN WESTMINSTER ABBEY

BY

H. C. BEECHING, D.LITT.

CANON OF WESTMINSTER

AND

ALEXANDER NAIRNE, M.A.

PROFESSOR OF HEBREW IN KING'S COLLEGE, LONDON

WILDSIDE PRESS

ADVERTISEMENT

THE lectures in this volume were delivered in Westminster Abbey during the Lent of 1906, on the foundation of Dame Joan Upton; who by her will dated Nov. 13, 1710, bequeathed a sum of £150 "to be invested, and the annual income thereof to be paid to five learned and orthodox divines of the Church of England, selected by the Dean, Sub-Dean, and Archdeacon of Westminster, for five sermons to be preached in the Collegiate Church of St. Peter on five Fridays in Lent for ever." The practice in recent years has been for a member of the Chapter to give the sermons, and to preach six instead of five; but on the present occasion, as the lecturer was anxious to leave London at the conclusion of his period of residence, he satisfied the requirement of the trust by preaching five sermons; and at the same time complied with the present custom of having a sermon on each of the six Fridays in Lent, by reviving the permission to nominate a "learned and orthodox divine" from outside the collegiate body. Professor Nairne accepted the invitation to conclude the course of lectures by taking for his subject the teaching about Atonement in the Epistle to the Hebrews.

It may be well to repeat the announcement made in the writer's previous volume of Westminster Lectures, that their purpose being catechetical and not critical, it has not been thought necessary to refer to authorities or to give reasons for preferring one interpretation to another on points which are in dispute. The lecturers have expressed their own views and convictions with a full sense of responsibility, and with a firm faith that a more thorough understanding of the doctrine of Holy Scripture on this most vital of all questions will unite believers more closely in their adherence to the Catholic faith, and recover many who from misconception have withdrawn themselves from the Christian fellowship.

H. C. B.

All Saints' Day, 1906.

OMP̄ SEMP̄ DS̄ QUI NULLI NOS INFERRE MAN-
DASTI QUOD NOBIS NON OPTAMUS INFERRI
PRAESTA QUAESUMUS UT NEC FINGAMUS ALIIS
NEC ALIORUM FICTIONIBUS INLUDAMUR PER.

Sacr. Leonian.

CONTENTS

LECTURE I

PAGE

THE EARLY RELIGION OF THE HEBREWS   I

For the study of Biblical doctrines the historical method pursued in this generation has great advantages, because it enables us to trace the development of a religious idea through all its stages, from its first manifestation up to its fulfilment in Christ. At first it may appear in a crude and materialistic form, but gradually—perhaps after being rejected in that shape—it becomes spiritualised. We find this to be the case with certain of the ideas which underlie the doctrine of Atonement, such as the solidarity of mankind, the desire for communion with God, and the demand for a Mediator. Accordingly the present lectures will follow the division of Old Testament history into the three great periods opening respectively with the Exodus, the Reformation under Josiah, and the Return from the Exile ; each of which is inaugurated by the delivery of a new code of law. In the first period the prescribed mode of worship is by sacrificial feasts at the traditional sanctuaries ; but in times of distress these are supplanted or supplemented by holocausts, of which the worshippers do not partake. The ideas underlying these two forms of sacrifice appear to be (1) communion, and (2) homage or propitiation ; the idea of reconciliation on account of sin has not arisen in this period because offences conceived as sin against God were held to be unpardonable and were punished with death. A third form of sacrifice in this period, that connected with the covenant, is important for the light it throws on the symbolism of sprinkling with blood, and consequently upon the sacrament of the new covenant.

        b

LECTURE II

The simple religion of the first period of Israelitish history, in which the priest and the judge were the same person, broke down in consequence of the social changes brought about by the Syrian wars and the growth of commerce. Religion became separated from morality by the increase of social wrongs, which, not being clearly recognised as sins against God, continued to be atoned for by payments to the sanctuary. This situation called out the great prophets of the eighth century B.C., with their message that Jehovah was essentially a God of righteousness, who must require righteousness in His worshippers and must punish injustice. The doctrine was proclaimed with characteristic differences, in the north by Amos and Hosea, and in the south by Isaiah and Micah. All alike denounce God's judgment on the people for their guilt ; but Hosea adds a promise of forgiveness to those who repent, and Isaiah looks forward to the time when the nation, purified by punishment, shall be governed in righteousness by a divinely-appointed Messiah-King. The practical outcome of the prophetic teaching was the abolition of local sanctuaries, and the restriction of sacrifice to the Temple at Jerusalem. The theoretical outcome was the revision of the Mosaic law in the Book of Deuteronomy, which dwells upon the righteousness and mercy of Jehovah, and the love which He requires from His people. Jeremiah, while finding occasion to repeat, in regard to the worship at Jerusalem, the warnings of preceding prophets that God requires righteousness rather than sacrifice, lays still greater stress than they on the inwardness of religion, and connects sin with the unfaithfulness of man's heart to God. The prophetic contribution to the doctrine of Atonement between man and God may be summed up under three heads : (1) the new knowledge they brought of God's character as a God of justice, mercy, and faithfulness ; (2) the disposition they required, corresponding to these

CONTENTS

The question left open by Amos and succeeding prophets, as to the ritual appropriate to the spiritual worship of God, was at length answered by Ezekiel, who drew up a reformed scheme of the traditional sacrifices, which laid a new emphasis on the idea of God's holiness and the necessity for approaching His presence free from the defilement of sin. The Levitical ceremonies, as practised in the second Temple, did not oppose the teaching of the prophets, either as to God's requirement of obedience to His moral law, or as to His readiness to forgive those who would repent. On the contrary, they helped to keep alive among the people the thought of God's care and holiness, and to implant the sense that man's sin can only be cancelled by God's grace. Ezekiel's new ritual of the sin offering, by which defilement was cleansed through the sprinkling of the blood of a holy victim (blood being understood to be the principle of life), was a counterpart to his new prophetic teaching that God would make man righteous by the gift of His Spirit. The cause of spiritual religion was further helped by the services of the synagogue begun during the exile, and also by the writing down of the Law and Prophetical books. The religious feeling of this period is reflected in many passages of the Psalter, which show how the doctrine of Atonement was interpreted by devout minds. An important influence in the direction of inward religion lay in the nation's experiences of suffering, interpreted as the punishment for sin. In one famous prophecy (Isaiah liii.) this suffering is declared to be vicarious and to have saving virtue.

CONTENTS

LECTURE IV

The teaching of the prophets had made it clear that Atonement between God and man presupposed a revelation of God's nature and will, and a power on man's part to respond to that revelation ; and, further, that both these elements of redemption must be the gifts of God's grace. In the time of the Pharisees the doctrine of divine grace had become overlaid, both as to the revelation of God's will and the response to it, on the one hand by a system of traditional rules which usurped the place of the divine commandments, and on the other by the merely outward obedience that these rules exacted. In opposition to the Pharisaic system our Lord recalled the prophetic teaching, and announced that in fulfilment of it He had come to "save sinners." He revealed to men the Fatherly love of God as a means to draw man's love in return and arouse penitence ; in order that He might forgive their sins and give them power to live a new life. This redemptive process is illustrated by various stories in the Gospels. But as hostility grew, our Lord foretold His murder at the hands of the priests and Pharisees ; and foretold also the large part His death was to play in the redemption of the people, according to the ancient prophecies, which spoke not only of the final establishment of God's righteous kingdom, but of the death of God's righteous servant as a sin-offering. The atoning efficacy of our Lord's death, according to His own teaching, includes (1) a power of convincing men of sin, (2) a power of attracting them to the Kingdom of God, and (3) a power of sending into men's hearts His own divine Spirit. The Atonement therefore presupposes and depends upon the Incarnation.

LECTURE V

St. Paul's doctrine of atonement is characteristically a doctrine of the free grace of God, being strongly defined against

CONTENTS

the Pharisaic doctrine of righteousness by human effort, for which he had zealously contended before his conversion. The Pharisaic theory, in his own experience, had broken down at the tenth Commandment, since he found himself unable to master the covetous desires of the flesh. It was the power of the Spirit of Jesus, vouchsafed to him at his conversion, which subdued the law in his members, and enabled him to live a life of righteousness. The pre-condition of receiving this righteousness, or the Spirit of Christ (for St. Paul uses both expressions synonymously) is faith in Jesus as the risen Lord. In his teaching about our Lord's death St. Paul sometimes repeats the doctrine of the Church (based on Isaiah liii.) as to its sacrificial character ; but more usually he avoids symbolic language and regards the Crucifixion as the consummation of a life of perfect obedience to the Father's will. By the obedience of the One, the many are made righteous. The advantage of the Passion to mankind he finds in man's power of identifying himself with it by faith, so as to die to his old nature and rise with Christ into a new life of Sonship with the Father. Hence this act of faith is generally expressed as a two-sided identification with Christ, in His death and resurrection. This theory of the Atonement rests upon the psychological basis of St. Paul's own experience at his conversion ; when "the law of the spirit of life in Christ Jesus" delivered him once for all from the law of sin and death ; but St. Paul's exhortations recognise that there may be Christians in whom conversion does not take the form of a sudden and complete death and resurrection ; but of a "mortifying" process. The theory that Christ by His death paid the penalty for man's breach of God's law is not Pauline.

LECTURE VI

Atonement in the Epistle to the Hebrews is represented in sacrificial language as access to God made possible for

man by Christ's offering of Himself, an offering which is
the one real Sacrifice because it was offered in the sphere
of the will. The author was a scholar of Jewish descent,
and he wrote to a small circle of scholarly men of the
same nation who were entering upon a crisis of faith ;
a sense of honour at a time of national danger combined
with their imperfect knowledge of the Person of Christ
to tempt them to abandon the new faith for the old. The
purpose of the epistle is twofold : to deepen their faith in
Christ, and to encourage them to hold fast to His side.
Since they are Jews the author takes for granted that they
are familiar with the Jewish principle of sacrifice—*i.e.*, that
in sacrifice life is not destroyed but offered to God, and
on this principle he bases the work of Christ. First,
as from a vantage point in heaven, he makes his friends
contemplate God manifesting Himself through the Eternal
Son, and suggests the question, " Is not this He whom
ye call your Lord ? " Then, setting them on earth again,
he shows them Jesus fulfilling in humiliation the glorious
destiny of man. Thus he deepens their thought about
their Lord, and prepares them to understand how One
thus human and divine may really have visited His people
as the true High Priest, standing on the Godward side of
men, fit to make atonement for them, and to lead them
into the presence of God. The ineffectual priesthood of
Aaron is seen, now the true Priest has appeared, to have
been the shadow of His priesthood. Yet the true priesthood has not been absent from history. In Melchizedek,
and in an Israelite priest-king like Melchizedek, the outline (not the shadow) of the true priesthood has been
visible. Now the outline has been filled up ; the true
Priest has made His offering of Himself; the blood-
shedding on Calvary has been the outward visible sign
of the offering of the indissoluble life in the presence of
God. Henceforth, on the basis of that Sacrifice, Jesus
Christ is present with the Father in Royal Priesthood.

This priestly work of Christ is brought into connexion
with men, and primarily with the readers of the Epistle,
by three lines of argument : (i) The sacrifice inaugurated
the New Covenant, and in the New Covenant a new

relationship with God began ; (ii) the entrance of Jesus into the presence of God opened the way to those who dare to follow Him by faith along that painful way of His flesh ; both these arguments would appeal with special force to the readers just at that time, for (iii) that Sacrifice was real because it was offered in the sphere of will, and in a like effort of will they are now summoned to unite themselves with Him. The Epistle with continually increasing insistence calls on them to follow their Lord, and ends with a collect in which its theology is summed up and its purpose culminates. The doctrine of Atonement is presented in this Epistle in a special form for particular men, but it is the same doctrine as that of the rest of Holy Scripture.

THE BIBLE DOCTRINE
OF ATONEMENT

LECTURE I

THE EARLY RELIGION OF THE HEBREWS

In making a study of the doctrine of Atonement, as it is found in the pages of Holy Scripture, it will be found profitable to proceed by the historical method. It has always been the belief of the Church that God's revelation to His people has been progressive—in many parts and in many ways, line upon line, and precept upon precept—and in our own day a closer investigation of the history of the Old Testament Scriptures has brought this principle of a progressive revelation more clearly into view. We can mark the stages in the development more clearly than was possible to our fathers. I propose, therefore, to take advantage of the clearer discrimination of periods which we owe to historical criticism, in order to mark in them the growing and deepening sense of the need of Atonement between God and His creature

I

man. The three great epochs in the history of Israel, of which in our investigation we must take account, are the Exodus, the Reformation under Josiah, and the Restoration after the Babylonian exile. These are, the first and last at any rate, cardinal epochs in the history of the people ; but they are also (and for us this is the important consideration) still more emphatically epochs in its spiritual development. To mark each of these great epochs we have in the Bible a code of laws formulated which sums up the spiritual teaching of each period. The first is found in certain chapters of Exodus (xx.-xxiv. and, again, xxxiv.),[1] the second in the Book of Deuteronomy, and the third in the Book of Leviticus and parts of the other Pentateuchal books. If you will regard those three great epochs, to borrow a useful figure, as "three knots upon the thread of revelation," the teaching of the Old Testament upon the subject of Atonement, as upon other subjects, will fall into order, and its gradual development will become manifest. The first three lectures will treat of these three preparatory stages ; then with the fourth we shall attempt to collect our Lord's own teaching on His passion as it is recorded in the Gospels, and so pass to consider the commentary of the apostles upon it.

---

[1] The variation between the "ten words" given in Exodus xx., as inscribed on the first tables of stone, and those of the second table given in Exodus xxxiv., would suggest that the Mosaic tradition, which underlay both, consisted of principles rather than commandments. These would be promulgated in somewhat different shapes at different times. Compare the further differences in Deuteronomy v.

The investigation will be found to exhibit one frequent principle of revelation—that a spiritual idea is first given to mankind in a very simple and, perhaps, a material shape; then, as religious insight quickens, it is challenged and discussed and repudiated, and, in consequence, this and that part of it is spiritualised and lifted to a higher plane, until at last the old idea is re-established, only not in its first material form, but in a form altogether spiritual. We shall find this principle illustrated in regard to certain great ideas which underlie the doctrine of Atonement. The first is the solidarity of mankind.

In early times, the tribe or nation is regarded as a single unit; as a single whole it sins and is punished, or repents and is forgiven. Then the difficulties of this conception emerge. For example, the question is raised—What proportion of righteous men will avail to save a community? Or, again, the question is asked—How can the suffering of a son for the sin of his father be reconciled with the justice of God? And by pondering such problems as these there dawns upon men's minds the truth of individual responsibility. You find the prophet Jeremiah definitely breaking with the old theory. "They shall say no more 'The fathers have eaten sour grapes, and the children's teeth are set on edge'; but every one shall die for his own iniquity. Every man that eateth the sour grape, his teeth shall be set on edge." But this new revelation is discovered presently not to be the whole truth. Experience shows that one man's sin does affect another; so does his repentance; and one man does suffer for another's sin, and this may avail towards the other's repentance. Thus, by degrees, the doctrine of the unity of men is raised from being a doctrine of union in one blood to being a doctrine of union in one spirit. The unity is first asserted, then denied, then asserted on a higher plane.

The same thing happens in the case of the doctrine of a mediator, which necessarily follows that of the solidarity of a race. When one man's sin was held to be a physical taint upon at least a large part of the community, certainly his immediate kindred (as we see in the story of Achan), it was also held that one man's active goodness might avail to justify his neighbours. Thus the zealous act of Phinehas in slaying the idolatrous Israelite is said to have covered the sin of the children of Israel. Similarly all the great prophets made intercession for the people, not so much as identifying themselves with them by an act of sympathy as representing them by sharing the same flesh and blood; and so covering Israel's sins from God's sight by what was also Israel's righteousness. But when the idea of national sin gave way before the growing idea of individual responsibility, it was revealed to the prophets that such intercession could no longer be accepted. The Word of the Lord came to Jeremiah (xv. 1)—"Though Moses and Samuel stood before me, yet my mind could not be toward this people; cast them out of my sight," and in a similar strain to Ezekiel (xiv. 20)— "Though Noah, Daniel, and Job were in it— as I live, saith the Lord God, they shall deliver

neither sons nor daughters ; they shall but deliver
their own souls by their righteousness." But
this was clearly not the last word. There is a
bond between man and man deeper than flesh
and blood—a bond of spirit—and if a mediator
could be found whose spirit was "life-giving,"
then from man to man would the sacred current
run, and by the one man's obedience the many
be made righteous. We pass, then, in the order
of evolution from a conception of responsibility
which allows mediation to one which denies it,
and then on from that to a reassertion of the
efficacy of mediatorial atonement in the sphere
of spirit.

Again, take the thought underlying the act
of sacrifice—that of the communion of men with
God, symbolised in the sharing of one sacred
blood. At first this communion is conceived as
something purely physical. God and man are
thought of as by nature akin ; the life they have
in common is held to be a natural life, and this
common life can be reinforced by sharing in
natural blood of a holy strain, because the life
is in the blood. This conception of sacrifice lies
behind all those idolatrous rites which had, right
up to the Exile, so much attraction for Israel.
With growing intelligence, of course, differences
between God and man are discerned. God can
no longer be conceived as eating bull's flesh and
drinking the blood of goats ; the bond of communion is rarefied by fire, and God is thought of
as delighting only in the savour of the sacrifice.
Then, as the thought of God's greatness and
righteousness and holiness deepens, the idea

that He can take any interest whatever in sacrifice
is absolutely denied.   God is defined as spirit
whom such material gifts cannot concern; and
sacrifice is explained as a mere act of homage,
or of self-renunciation, or of self-purification.
In other words, sacrifice passes from being a
physical link uniting man with God to become
a means or a symbol of spiritualising man so
that he may approach God.   In this way the
communion of man with God becomes gradually
realised as something essentially spiritual; and
the Levitical system itself becomes an attempt to
preserve this more spiritual idea which had come
to expression in the Exile.   Then the original
idea of sacrificial communion with God, after
being denied on the physical plane, is reasserted
on the spiritual plane in the Christian feast, in
which the one holy and divine life is still the
means of communion.

Just one word more of preface.   We are most
fortunate in possessing in our English tongue
the beautiful word "atonement," formed from
the old phrase "to be at one," which keeps before
our minds what is the very essence of true
religion, the communion between God and man,
without committing us by any figure of speech
to any theory as to how this communion was
won or must be preserved.   A great deal of
popular misunderstanding of theology is always
arising from pressing too closely the original
sense of words, which at the best are only
metaphors applied to subjects far too high for
them.   In theology more than in most subjects
it is well to recollect the warning of Bacon,

" Men believe that their reason governs words ; but it is also true that words react on the understanding " (*Nov. Organ.*, Aph. lix.).

Let us pass on now to our investigation, and let us consider to-day the relations of men with God as we can trace them in the first period of Israelitish history after the settlement in Canaan. The code of laws of that period is given in Exodus xxi.-xxiii., and again in chapter xxxiv. If you will turn to that body of customs you will see that the line between civil and religious precepts is not clearly marked. The code passes from directions how to make an altar to directions about Hebrew slavery, and from rules about loans and deposits to the law of first-fruits. Moreover, in cases of theft the rule is, " For every matter of trespass, whether it be for ox, for ass, for sheep, for raiment, or for any manner of lost thing whereof one saith ' This is it,' the cause of both parties shall come before God ; he whom God shall condemn shall pay double unto his neighbour" (xxii. 9)—that is to say, the priest at the sanctuary is to decide. So again in cases of homicide it is laid down (Exod. xxi. 12, 13), " He that smiteth a man so that he die shall surely be put to death. And if a man lie not in wait I will appoint thee a place whither he shall flee [that is, the sanctuary], but if a man come presumptuously upon his neighbour to slay him with guile, thou shalt take him from mine altar that he may die."

Such laws make it clear that the legislation is intended for a very simple society, in which the thought of God's immediate providence is very

strong. But what is His character? He is a
God who loves justice, that is made clear (as in
xxiii. 6-8); and again, He is a God who loves
mercy. The regulations for compassion to
strangers, widows, and fatherless are emphatic
(Exod. xxii. 21, 24). And the Sabbath is ordained
"That thine ox and thine ass may rest, and the
son of thine handmaid and the stranger may be
refreshed." It is in such regulations as these
that the two great notes of the character of
Jehovah, His justice and His mercy, were first
impressed upon the Children of Israel.

We proceed, then, to ask, What was the prescribed mode of worship? How were the people
to present themselves before God? The answer
is, By sacrifice. The regulations are very simple.
There was to be an altar of earth, or of unhewn
stone, and on this were to be sacrificed what
the English Bible calls "burnt offerings and
peace offerings" of sheep and oxen. Where
these altars are to be is not laid down, but the
general promise is given, "In all places where
I record my name, I will come unto thee and I
will bless thee." We know from the history
where the greater sanctuaries, as a matter of
fact, were. They were in places consecrated by
the traditions of the ancestors of the race—
Abraham, Isaac, and Jacob—Hebron and Beersheba, Mizpah and Bethel, and also in places
where, in the subsequent history, God had revealed His presence to great judges or prophets
—Joshua's Gilgal, Gideon's Ophrah, Samuel's
Ramah, Elijah's Carmel. These sanctuaries were
for many centuries the centre of the religious

life of the people. Thither they went to have their hard cases tried. There were preserved stories of Jehovah's dealings with His people, the stories of the patriarchs and the judges, and the great prophets, Samuel and Elijah and Elisha, and there were held the great religious festivals of sacrifice. To one or other of these sanctuaries the Israelite was to make pilgrimage on three stated occasions (Ex. xxiii. 14) : "Three times thou shalt keep a feast unto me in the year—the feast of unleavened bread shalt thou keep, and the feast of harvest, the first-fruits of thy labours which thou sowest in thy field, and the feast of ingathering at the end of the year."

Notice, for it is important if we are to understand the Hebrew religion of this period, that the three great annual sacrifices are described as "feasts"—"Three times thou shalt keep a feast unto me." To illustrate what took place at one of these sacrificial feasts we may turn to the first Book of Samuel, chap. ix., where the story is told of the anointing of Saul to be king. Saul and his servant go to inquire of Samuel the seer about some lost asses, and as they climb up to the city they meet certain maidens, and ask, " Is the seer here ? " And the reply is, " He is ; he is before thee ; make haste now, for he is come to-day into the city ; for the people have a sacrifice to-day in the high place : as soon as ye be come into the city ye shall find him before he go up to the high place to eat ; for the people will not eat till he come, because he doth bless the sacrifice ; and afterwards they eat that be bidden." And you will recollect that, in the

2

sequel, Saul is made chief guest at the sacrificial feast, and the story concludes, " So Saul did eat with Samuel that day."

We are not told what was the special reason of the gathering. There were thirty persons present, and it may have been the annual feast or sacrifice of a particular clan—such as we read of later when David excused himself from Saul's court on the pretext of attending the yearly sacrifice of his house at Bethlehem (1 Sam. xx. 6). In the story itself nothing is said of what to us would seem the only religious part of the festival —the act of sacrifice—except that Samuel blessed it. In this phrase certain ritual acts are, no doubt, implied ; what they were we know from the only ritual directions in this earliest code of laws. They were two—" Thou shalt not offer the blood of my sacrifice with leavened bread, neither shall the fat of my sacrifice remain until the morning." On the prohibitions connected with these rules I need not dwell, but the rules are that the blood and the fat are to be offered, as being the most precious part of the victim. This—we may say it reverently—is Jehovah's share in the common feast. So, you may re-member, the worshippers at the sanctuary of Shiloh are represented as saying to the priest's servant, " Let them not fail to burn the fat at once " (1 Sam. ii. 16). The whole ceremony, therefore, was a common feast, at which Jehovah took part with His worshippers. It is not that the sacrifice was concluded with a feast. The feast, being held at the sanctuary, was itself the religious action, the sacrifice. This point of

view is brought home to us by a saying of Hosea
(ix. 4), when he foretold the Captivity of Israel—
" their sacrifices shall be as the bread of mourners,
for the food shall be merely to satisfy their
appetite ; it shall not come into the house of the
Lord." As we might say of our Christian feast,
it shall be merely bread and wine, not consecrated
for sacrament. It is, in fact, our Christian feast
that makes it possible for us to understand the
sacrificial feasts of the Hebrews. St. Paul, in
his letter to the Corinthians (x. 14, 21), enforces
this comparison : " Behold Israel after the flesh
—have not they which eat of the sacrifices their
fellowship with the altar ? " that is, with God.
And he goes on to compare a Jew sitting at a
sacrificial feast or a heathen at a heathen feast
with a Christian at the Eucharist, in the point
that they are all keeping fellowship with their
deities.   " The things which the Gentiles sacrifice,
they sacrifice to demons and not to God, and I
would not that ye should have *fellowship* with
demons. Ye cannot *partake of the table* of the
Lord and of the table of demons." When we
read, then, of the feast that Samuel made at
Shiloh, or the sacrifice at Gilgal when Saul was
made king and the people " rejoiced greatly," or
the more domestic occasion when Elkanah with
his wives and sons and daughters sacrificed and
feasted as a family in Shiloh, or even that de-
plorable feast at Sinai when Aaron made the
molten calf to represent Jehovah, and sacrificed,
and " the people sat down to eat and drink and
rose up to play," we have the regular type
of Hebrew worship in early days. It is well

expressed by the phrase of Exodus (xxiv. 11), "they saw God and did eat and drink."

But no religion can be merely one of joy. Trouble comes to every one; and the Hebrews, we know, had trouble enough from their enemies round about. We must go on to ask, then, When they sought the Lord in trouble, did they approach Him with any special kind of sacrifice? Keeping to the story of Samuel, which we have used, so far, for our illustrations, we may turn to the account of what happened at Mizpah when the people were suddenly attacked by the Philistines (1 Sam. vii. 8-10): "And the children of Israel said to Samuel, Cease not to cry unto the Lord our God for us, that He will save us out of the hand of the Philistines. And Samuel took a sucking lamb, and offered it for a whole burnt offering unto the Lord: and Samuel cried unto the Lord for Israel; and the Lord answered him. And as Samuel was offering up the burnt offering, the Philistines drew near to battle against Israel: but the Lord thundered with a great thunder on that day upon the Philistines, and discomfited them."

Here we have a sacrifice of another type, not a feast, for the people had no share in the victim; it was offered whole upon the altar. And we find this same sort of sacrifice offered at other times of crisis or of special solemnity. What did it signify? We can explain it best on the analogy of gifts to a king. It is a form of homage, corresponding, on special occasions, to the regular gifts of firstlings which the law prescribed. It expressed the humility and faith and duty of the worshipper, and his desire to have his petition granted ; it was, in a word, intended to propitiate. It may well be that, among the heathen nations round, there had been originally in these holocausts the idea of providing a special feast for their gods, by way of assuaging their wrath ; of which early and barbarous idea there remains a strange survival even in the sacred books themselves in the expression " The Lord smelled a sweet savour," which even St. Paul quotes. But it was only the phrase, not the idea, that survived among the Hebrews. The true idea comes out in that saying of King David at the threshing-floor of Araunah—" Neither will I offer burnt offerings unto the Lord my God of that which doth cost me nothing." The motive which still prompts religious people to give, or to vow, churches, or the ornaments of churches, as acts of prayer or thanksgiving, was the motive that underlay these whole burnt offerings. On some occasions we find these burnt offerings combined with the sacrificial feast. For example, it is said (Exod. xviii. 12) : " And Jethro, Moses' father-in-law, took a burnt offering and sacrifices for God ; and Aaron came and all the elders of Israel to eat bread with Moses' father-in-law before God."

We see, then, how the sense of satisfaction in the divine protection, and the sense of deprecation of the calamities that threaten, both receive expression in the sacrificial rites of the early Hebrew religion ; but what do we find about the sense of sin ? How was that expressed in terms of ritual ; and the atonement that the sense of sin cries out for—how was that expressed ?

Before that question can be answered, we must bear in mind that early religion took more account of the tribe than of the individual, unless he was a representative individual—king, or judge, or prophet. The sacrificial feasts were expressions of the national or tribal spirit, proud of being, or desirous to be, under the protection of the Lord of Hosts; solicitous or thankful for the fruits of the earth in their season ; and the whole burnt offerings were offered by representative men on behalf of the people. The individual Israelite had hardly yet come into personal relation with Jehovah, except through his clan. The offences possible for him to commit—theft, homicide, and so forth—so far as they were not avenged by the wronged man's own kin, were assessed at the sanctuary in terms of a fine; but though assessed, as it were, before God, the assessments were customary, and there was no clear and practical sense that such wrongs were offences against God. The cry that we hear from the Psalmist—"Against Thee, Thee only, have I sinned," would have been unintelligible to the ordinary Israelite in the days of Samuel ; as we can see from the words of Eli to his sons : —"If one man sin against another, God shall judge him; but if a man sin against the Lord, who shall entreat for him ? " A sin against another man was not regarded as a sin against God, although it was a breach of divine law ; for sins against God there was no atonement. We see this in the few recorded instances of sins which are regarded as sins against Jehovah. The offence of the Israelites at Sinai in making and worshipping the molten calf is so described, and no atonement is allowed for it. (Exod. xxxii. 30.) The sin of Achan in stealing some of the spoil of Jericho which had been cursed is characterised as a sin against the Lord God of Israel, and it was punished with death. Saul, again, though punctilious on all points of ritual—refusing to let the people eat their spoil till the blood had been poured out at the altar, and enforcing a curse even against his own son—is described as having sinned unpardonably himself in sparing the Amalekite King Agag, when the whole kingdom had been put under ban.

It is quite clear, therefore, that a development of spiritual religion must proceed in two directions—on the one hand it must bring all wrongs wrought by man against man into the rank of sins against God, and on the other it must deny God's unforgivingness to those who, whatever their fault, sincerely repent. That is the work which was accomplished—for those who would receive the revelation—by the great prophets of the eighth century, of whom I shall speak in the next lecture.

In conclusion, I would ask your attention to one other early form of sacrifice, which has an important bearing on the subject of Atonement— I mean the Covenant sacrifice. It is thus described in Exod. xxiv. 4-8 :—" And Moses wrote all the words of the Lord, and rose up early in the morning and builded an altar under the mount, and twelve pillars according to the twelve tribes of Israel. And he sent young men of the children of Israel which offered burnt offerings and sacrificed peace offerings of oxen unto the Lord. And Moses took half of the blood and put it in basins ; and half of the blood he sprinkled on the altar. And he took the book of the covenant, and read in the audience of the people ; and they said, All that the Lord hath spoken will we do, and be obedient. And Moses took the blood, and sprinkled it on the people, and said, Behold the blood of the covenant which the Lord hath made with you concerning all these words."

What is the meaning of sprinkling blood upon the altar and upon the people ? We shall understand if we remember that the blood was held to be the seat of life, and so was especially holy. The Hebrews were forbidden to eat it ; it was poured out as an offering to Him from whom all life comes. To put the same blood, therefore, upon two persons was to unite them in the bond of a common life. It was thus the strongest possible symbol of communion and fellowship. And if we ask whose the blood is supposed to be in this case, it is as if we asked, What is the life into which the people are initiated ? and we can but answer, that (whether consciously realised or not) the common life must be the life of Him who took the other into covenant. For the covenant is not between two equals. The people say, " All that the Lord hath spoken will we do, and be obedient." And then Moses sprinkles the blood upon them, the symbol of a new and holy life, according to the new law.

This idea of a covenant between Jehovah and Israel—"I will be their God, and they shall be my people"—has been called[1] "the fundamental redemptive idea" of the people of Israel, —"the frame in which the development of their religion grew," as they came gradually to understand what was implied in the nature of God and in their relation to Him. At first—as we can see from the history—the contract was considered by the people to be something of this sort: that Jehovah, who had first made Himself known to them as the Lord of Hosts, and had brought them out of slavery and given them the land of promise, would protect them with His almighty arm in all their dangers and necessities, especially from their enemies round about, and give them decisions through His priests and prophets; while they, for their part, would bring Him their firstfruits, whether of men or cattle or corn, and keep His Sabbaths and His feasts. That is roughly the point we have reached to-day. Let us look forward and see, in a few words, what is the further history of this idea of the Covenant.

The first great lesson the people had to learn was that their covenant with Jehovah forbade the tolerance of any rival worship such as that of Baal. "Jehovah was a jealous God." This is the lesson connected especially with the mission of the prophet Elijah—"Jehovah, He is the God." Then came the mission of the eighth-century prophets, who dwelt on the "holiness" of Jehovah, and expounded this holiness in terms not of ceremonial jealousy, but of civil righteous-

[1] *Theology of the Old Testament*, by A. B. Davidson, p. 238.

3

ness, with unexpected consequences to the other party to the covenant. " You only have I known of all the families of the earth ; therefore I will punish you for your iniquity "[1]—a terrible paradox for a covenant relation. " I have chosen you ; I love you ; therefore I will punish you." This prophetic view of the Covenant is brought to a point in the statement of Deuteronomy [2] that the Covenant, as made originally at Horeb, was made upon the basis of the ten great ethical commandments, and that therefore the love of the people for Jehovah, which was to answer His love of Israel, must express itself in keeping these commandments. But prophet after prophet sadly confesses that Israel has broken the Covenant, has not kept the Commandments, and must be punished. Is there anything more that God can do ? There is one thing : He can give them the power to keep His covenant, or, as Jeremiah expresses it,[3] He can make a new covenant with them, and write His law this time, not on tables of stone, but upon their hearts.

And so, at the Last Supper, before His death, the Lord Jesus took the cup, and blessed and gave it to His disciples, and said, " Drink ye all of this ; for this is my Blood of the new Covenant which is shed for many." When the old Covenant was made, the blood of the divine sacrifice was sprinkled upon the people as a sign that they were taken up into the holy life ; under the new Covenant the symbol has become a reality, and the life of Christ Jesus becomes the very life of His people.

[1] Amos iii. 2.   [2] Deut. ix. 9, etc.   [3] xxxi. 31.

LECTURE II

THE EPOCH OF THE PROPHETS

In the early days of Hebrew religion, when Jehovah was regarded by the average Israelite as his national God, in much the same sense as Chemosh was the god of the Moabites—the idea of Atonement could not receive any very deep interpretation. The regular sacrifices were rather assertions of the fact, and rejoicings in the fact that Jehovah was their God, than attempts to conciliate His favour; and so they naturally took the form of feasts; and although defeat in war or destruction by pestilence would at once incline them to suppose that Jehovah had in some way been offended, and a priest or prophet would be consulted, and burnt offerings made for propitiation, yet the normal religious life would be one of contentment, without much searching of heart. And such a state of things might continue without raising any serious protest from the better spirits of the nation, as long as the customary morality of the people held its ground —as long, that is to say, as the public spirit of the various tribal or village communities was strong enough to enforce the time-honoured laws against robbery and other forms of oppression;

and that would be as long as men remained much on a level in point of social importance. But, with the decay of agriculture through a long period of war, and also with the growth of commerce, wealth becomes more and more unevenly distributed (as we know in our present world), and customary sanctions are no longer found strong enough to bind the conscience of the man who has the power to do wrong.

That was, roughly, the position in Israel in the days of Jeroboam II., when the great step forward was taken in religion which we are to consider in this lecture. How did it come about? Not as we might think it ought to have come about, from the professed interpreters of the divine law at the local sanctuaries. It was an unfortunate consequence of the system by which civil offences were expiated by money fines paid to the priests that the richer classes came to have practically a licence to do whatever they could pay for, and the priest had a direct interest in encouraging these fines. In the terrible words of Hosea,[1] instead of teaching the people the law of God, the priests " set their hearts on their iniquity," and so the dramatic scene in which the great period of Jewish prophecy opens is the confronting of the chief priest in the royal sanctuary at Bethel by a countryman from the south, upon whom, after so long a time, God sent once more the spirit of Elijah :—" And Amaziah said unto Amos, O thou seer, go, flee thee away into the land of Judah, and there eat bread, and prophesy

[1] iv. 8 : cf. 2 Kings xii. 16. See Robertson Smith's *Prophets of Israel*, pp. 100 ff.

there. But prophesy not again any more at Bethel, for it is the king's sanctuary, and a royal house. Then answered Amos, and said to Amaziah, I was no prophet nor a son of the prophets, but a herdman and a dresser of syca-more trees ; and the Lord took me from following the flock, and the Lord said unto me, Go prophesy unto my people Israel" (Amos vii. 12).

The denial of Amos that he was one of the sons of the prophets reminds us that ever since the time of Samuel there had been companies of prophets connected with the sanctuaries, who worshipped God after a dervish fashion and gave divinations (1 Sam. ix. 6-8, x. 5, 6 ; Micah iii. 11 ; Amos vii. 12) ; but of whatever use they may once have been in stimulating men to the worship of God, they had long ceased to be of service ; and, like the priests, they had become attached to the court, and, for the most part, merely echoed the wishes of their masters, as we learn from the story of Ahab and Micaiah. Those whom we henceforward rank as prophets were individuals called from every sort of social rank to deliver some special message that God had spoken to their hearts ; and they are as far as possible from repro-ducing any of the uncontrolled enthusiasm which was a mark of the established prophetic order.

What, then, we must ask, was this new message of Amos and the prophets who succeeded him ? They saw that the land was full of devotion of a sort—fuller, indeed, than ever it had been before, for the Northern Kingdom had been fortunate in the war against Damascus. But they saw also that the land was full of wickedness, especially in the form of oppression ; and they met the situation in this way :

They reminded the people that Jehovah's relation with Israel was not a natural relation, to which He was in any sense obliged, but one entered into in sheer loving-kindness when He rescued them from slavery in Egypt. The cry of the Israelite was, " Is not the Lord among us ? No evil can happen to us ! " " No ! " said the prophets, " God is not necessarily among you ; He may even be bringing up an army against you. God's relation with you is a covenant relation, God choosing the people and giving a law which you undertook to obey."

They reminded the people that Jehovah was before all else a God of righteousness, who loved righteousness and hated iniquity ; this was His character ; righteousness, therefore, must be what He requires of men ; and nothing else can satisfy or please Him. One or two of the prophets go so far as to say that He has never commanded anything else ; that the original covenant of Jehovah with the people was given upon the basis of the Ten Commandments, which are commandments of righteousness, and do not require sacrifice. But all of them protest against the absurdity of offering a sacrificial bribe to the righteous Judge of all the world, as though it could induce Him not to punish iniquity. They re-echo that great word of the father of the nation, " Must not the Judge of all the earth do right ? " [1] and that great word of the first of the prophets, " Behold, to obey is better than sacrifice." [2]

[1] Gen. xviii. 25.   [2] I Sam. xv. 22.

Popular religion, therefore, according to the prophets, was on a wrong tack altogether. The people were acting as though they kept within the Covenant by performing the regular sacrifices with expense and enthusiasm, whereas the one only thing that Jehovah cared for, and looked for, was obedience to the Ten Commandments—in one word, righteous dealing. To us this identification of religion with righteousness is so familiar that we can hardly imagine a time when it could be preached almost as a new revelation from God, and be received with incredulity as a hard saying. But we have only to turn to the history of the prophets to assure ourselves that they were speaking what the people found it difficult to receive. This is how Amos denounces the sacrificial feasts at Bethel and the other sanctuaries :

" Thus saith the Lord unto the house of Israel, Seek ye me, and ye shall live, but seek not Bethel, nor enter into Gilgal, and pass not to Beersheba [three of the most famous sanctuaries], for Gilgal shall surely go into captivity, and Bethel shall come to nought. Seek Jehovah, and ye shall live, ye who turn justice to wormwood, and cast down righteousness to the earth. . . . Forasmuch, therefore, as ye trample upon the poor, and take exactions from him of wheat, ye have built houses of hewn stone, but ye shall not dwell in them ; ye have planted pleasant vineyards, but ye shall not drink the wine thereof; for I know how manifold are your transgressions, and how mighty are your sins; ye that afflict the just, that take a bribe, and that turn aside the needy in the gate [that is, at the judgment-seat]. Seek good, and not evil, that ye may live; and so Jehovah, the God of hosts, shall be with you, as ye say " (v. 4).

There is no misunderstanding that appeal; it says simply, God wants righteousness from you, not sacrifice. You must seek God by seeking good. Amos expressly asserts that God, when He gave the Law to Moses in the wilderness of Sinai, gave no directions for sacrifice (v. 25). He implies that the Israelites did not adopt the custom of sacrifice till they reached Canaan. And he makes his most effective point by asserting that other nations had been punished not for idolatry, but for unrighteousness, and then asking how Israel, whose privileges in the Ten Commandments were greater, could hope to be spared, when, notwithstanding their privileges, they were equally unrighteous.

Hosea, who prophesied a few years later than Amos, brings against the people the same charge: "The Lord hath a controversy with the inhabitants of the land, because there is no truth, nor mercy, nor knowledge of God in the land. There is nought but swearing and breaking faith, and killing, and stealing, and committing adultery." He makes also the same attack upon the ritual religion: "I desire kindness, and not sacrifice, and the knowledge of God more than burnt offerings." This term, "the knowledge of God," which we thus meet for the first time, coupled with the corresponding term "kindness," or "love," shows us that Hosea looked at religion from a point of view much nearer to our own even than that of Amos. He sketches the history of God's loving care of the people whom He had chosen, and then employs the argument we are so familiar with in St. John's words—" Brethren, if God so loved us we ought also to love one another." His appeal is in two parts: (1) " Let us follow on to know the Lord," to know Him as what He is, a tender Father who has always loved Israel; and (2) knowing Him, let us act as His children, by dutiful affection to Him, and to all our brethren within His covenant.

We gather from the prophecies of Amos and Hosea that in some places the worship of the Israelitish sanctuaries was like that of the heathen Canaanites—not only in such outward features as sacred images and emblems, but also in the encouragement it gave to drunkenness and licentiousness; but without pressing points like this, which may not have been universal, it is sufficient to recognise with them the solemn fact that while the people were worshipping God with sacrifice He was bringing the Assyrians against their land as a punishment for their disobedience to His moral commandments. We cannot mistake the sense of such a passage as this: " I hate, I despise your sacrificial feasts; I will take no delight in your solemn assemblies. Yea, though ye offer me your burnt offerings and meat offerings, I will not accept them; neither will I regard the peace offerings of your fed beasts. Take thou away from me the noise of thy songs; for I will not hear the melody of thy viols. But let justice run down as waters, and righteousness as a mighty stream " (Amos v. 21).

4

If we ask, Did Amos offer the people a chance
to be reconciled to God? the answer is not
quite clear. He sees the judgment coming, and
does not hint that it can be stayed. But he
looks beyond it to a righteous remnant sifted
out by captivity; in much the same spirit as
Elijah had been assured at Horeb that Jehovah
would spare all the knees that had not bowed
to Baal. We have, therefore, in this teaching
of Amos one of the two great advances in
spiritual religion that we saw to be necessary
—that all wrongs done by man to man shall be
seen to be sins against God. For the second,
the promise of God's forgiveness to those who
repent, we must go to Hosea, who sees that if
God is indeed Israel's " Father," there can be
no question of His readiness to forgive : " How
can I give thee up, Ephraim? How can I cast
thee away, Israel ? My heart burns within me ;
My compassion is kindled. I will not execute
the fierceness of my wrath ; I will not turn to
destroy thee, for I am God and not man—the
Holy One in the midst of thee" (xi. 8). " I will
heal their backslidings ; I will love them freely "
(xiv. 4). As we know, the Northern Kingdom
found no place of repentance. But the lessons
preached in the North by Amos and Hosea
were echoed in Jerusalem by a greater prophet
still—the prophet Isaiah; and there they bore
lasting fruit for the world. Every one knows
the familiar passages in which Isaiah denounces
the moral offences of his people on the one
hand, and the multiplication of sacrifices on the
other :

" To what purpose is the multitude of your
sacrifices unto me ? saith the Lord. I am full
of the burnt offerings of rams, and the fat of
fed beasts; and I delight not in the blood of
bullocks, or of lambs, or of he-goats. When ye
come to appear before me, who hath required
this at your hands, to trample my courts ? Bring
no more vain oblations ; incense is an abomina-
tion unto me ; new moon and sabbath, the calling
of assemblies—I cannot away with iniquity and
the solemn meeting. Your hands are full of
blood. Wash you, make you clean; put away
the evil of your doings from before mine eyes ;
cease to do evil, learn to do well ; seek judgment,
relieve the oppressed, judge the fatherless, plead
for the widow " (i. 11-17).

The distinction of Isaiah from his predecessors
is twofold—first, that he has a clearer vision
than they both of the judgment impending,
and of God's merciful intention to purify the
nation by its means, and not to destroy it wholly.
He looks forward to a time when justice shall
be impartially administered—" I will restore thy
judges as at the first, and thy counsellors as
at the beginning : afterward thou shalt be called
'the city of righteousness, the faithful city.' "
Secondly, he was a man of affairs with a practical
policy, and so contributed in some degree to
effect necessary reforms in the nation ; partly
by his influence with King Hezekiah following
upon the great deliverance from Sennacherib
which the prophet had foretold, but still more
by the fact that he gathered about him a circle
of disciples, which, as they grew in numbers,

became in themselves the promise and germ of a reformed people.

Summing up, then, the teaching of these great prophets, Amos, Hosea, and Isaiah—and the same lessons are preached even more simply and emphatically by Isaiah's contemporary Micah —we may say that the prophets denounce Jehovah's anger against Israel and Judah for their unrighteousness in the social life of every day, and look forward to a time when, after the punishment of the evil-doers, a remnant shall repent and accept God's righteous law and obey it. The Atonement, or reconciliation with God, to which they look forward, is in a righteous kingdom under God's protection, ruled by a prince of David's house, a man after God's own heart. " There shall come forth a shoot out of the stock of Jesse, and the spirit of Jehovah shall rest upon him, and his delight shall be in the fear of the Lord; and with righteousness shall he judge the poor, and reprove with equity for the meek of the earth. And righteousness shall be the girdle of his loins, and faithfulness the girdle of his reins " (Isa. xi.). Such is to be the kingdom of Messiah, in which man shall be at peace with God, because "the earth shall be full of the knowledge of the Lord." The Atonement, therefore, to which the prophets look forward is quite independent of sacrificial rites; these they regard only as a national symbol of the people's service, not prescribed by God, which, as a matter of fact, has distracted them from their true service; the only Atonement possible with a God of righteousness must come, they say, from righteous conduct. This is how the conclusion of the whole matter is set down in Isaiah's final prophecy: "Who among us shall dwell with the devouring fire? Who among us shall dwell with everlasting burnings?"—[*i.e.*, with God, whose holiness shall burn up everything unholy]. And the answer is: "He that walketh righteously, and speaketh uprightly; he that despiseth the gains of fraud, that shaketh his hands from holding bribes; that stoppeth his ears from hearing of blood, and shutteth his eyes from looking on evil" (xxxiii. 14).

What was the practical outcome of Isaiah's mission in Jerusalem? Whether his influence was potent enough to ensure for a time the appointment of just judges—as, on one occasion, he was certainly able to replace the wicked treasurer Shebna by Eliakim, we cannot say; but such influence could not be permanent. Reform in social life, though it may come from the influence of a single man, must depend upon reform in national ideals. But one great practical change was made by Hezekiah, which, although it provoked resentment, and was undone by his successor, Manasseh, was finally established by Josiah. The worship of the local sanctuaries, which had never shaken itself free from Canaanite influences, was suppressed, and sacrifice was restricted to the Temple at Jerusalem, where it could be under strict supervision. The Book of Deuteronomy, the discovery of which during some repairs in the Temple, in the eighteenth year of Josiah, formed the starting-point and model of Josiah's reformation, is

practically the Mosaic Code, written out with
careful explanations from this new point of view.
It must have been composed under the influence
of Isaiah's teaching, either at the end of Hezekiah's reign or during the reign of Manasseh.
It rehearses the ancient rules about the annual
sacrificial feasts, with the necessary changes to
adapt them to the new circumstances of the single
sanctuary ; but it follows the older code of laws
in laying by far the greater stress on the moral
law of conduct, reproducing all the old kindly
laws, some of them in a still more humane form.
But the most striking feature of the book—due
to the recent prophetic teaching—is the insistence upon the spirituality of God, the unity
and uniqueness of God, and, above all, the love
of God for Israel, which calls for Israel's love
in return.   Each of the great prophets of the
eighth century contributed some element to the
conception of Jehovah that we find portrayed
in the pages of Deuteronomy.   Isaiah's vision of
the majesty of God, before whom the cherubim
cover their faces, and whose Godhead fills the
whole earth, and Amos's sublime sense of the
righteousness of God, as the very principle of
the universe, have each contributed to it ; but
even more prominent than these is the thought,
which formed the revelation to Hosea, of the
great love of God, which could be satisfied with
nothing else than man's answering love.   The
characteristic tone of Deuteronomy comes out in
that great sentence which our Lord quoted as
the " first commandment of the law "—" Hear, O
Israel : the Lord our God is one Lord ; and thou

shalt love the Lord thy God with all thine heart, and with all thy soul, and with all thy might;" the reason being that God had loved them and done great things for them, and wished them to be like Himself, righteous as He was righteous, merciful as He was merciful; "a God that regardeth not persons, nor taketh reward, that doth execute the judgment of the fatherless and widow and loveth the stranger."

The prophet we must next take notice of, one who speaks upon the basis of this reformed religion, was Jeremiah. And we may wonder what general truth about God's righteousness remained yet to urge after the prophecies of his great predecessors. But the fact was that Jeremiah found urgent need to repeat their lessons because the old superstitions about sacrifice, although banished from the local sanctuaries, found an even intenser life in connection with the Temple at Jerusalem. When we remember that the great event which gave Isaiah his popularity and his power was the destruction of Sennacherib's army, we can readily understand how the inviolability of the Temple on Mount Zion, with its sacrificial worship of Jehovah, became a main article of belief to the Jewish people. And so Jeremiah finds it necessary to repeat, with even greater emphasis than his predecessors, that God's original Covenant with the people of Israel was based upon the Ten Commandments, and excluded sacrifice altogether. "I spake not unto your fathers, nor commanded them in the day that I brought them out of the land of Egypt, concerning burnt offering and sacrifice; but this thing I commanded them, saying, Hearken unto my voice" (vii. 22; cf. Deut. v. 2, 22). And though he does not say that he wishes the Temple in Jerusalem to follow the local sanctuaries to destruction, he does say, and he nearly lost his life for saying it, that the sacrifices offered in the Temple were no more protection to the city and the people than the sacrifices had been in the sanctuaries, because in no place could sacrifice be accepted in lieu of a good life.

"Will ye steal, murder, commit adultery, and swear falsely . . . and come and stand before me in this house, which is called by my name, and say, We are delivered, that ye may do all these abominations?" "Is this house, which is called by my name, become a den of robbers in your eyes? Behold I, even I, have seen it, saith the Lord. But go ye now unto my place which was in Shiloh, where I caused my name to dwell at the first, and see what I did to it for the wickedness of my people Israel. And now, because ye have done all these works, saith the Lord, and I spake unto you, rising up early and speaking, but ye heard not; and I called you, but ye answered not; therefore will I do unto this house which is called by my name, wherein ye trust, and unto the place which I gave to you and your fathers, as I have done to Shiloh" (vii. 9-15).

But, apart from this necessary repetition of the main prophetic ideas about the true worship of God, as consisting in the moral duties of justice and mercy, Jeremiah brings into still

clearer view than his predecessors had done
that these moral duties depended upon religion.
"Thou shalt love the Lord thy God." He is
full of the sense that sins arise from the unfaithfulness to God of man's hard heart. It is
man's heart that God looks to—"the Lord
searcheth the heart"—and man's heart proves
"deceitful above all things, and desperately sick."
And so Jeremiah looked forward to a time when
Jehovah should write His laws on the people's
hearts, so that they could not choose but obey
Him. This hope is the final word of prophecy.
Let us sum up, then, shortly the advance made by
the great Prophets in the doctrine of Atonement.

The great advance which drew with it all
others was an advance in the knowledge of God.
Before the prophetic period Jehovah was regarded
for the most part as the God of the nation and
the owner of the soil, who gave them corn and
wine, in whose presence, therefore, they rejoiced
at the appropriate seasons. He was also the
God of their armies, who gave them victory
against their foes. He was also the God who
gave them laws and decisions—"words" to guide
their lives. But with the prophets a call came
to the people to "know the Lord," to consider
His dealings with them, and to understand His
character, of which these dealings were a manifestation. "My people doth not know, Israel
doth not consider"—that is the complaint we
hear through the lips of Isaiah ; the sins against
which the prophets protest came, in great measure,
from confusing Jehovah with the Canaanite
Baals—which would have been impossible if they

had known Jehovah's true nature. What, then, is the character of God as the prophets reveal it ? It is summed up in the word " righteousness." Jehovah was a righteous Judge, and the Israelite who bore false witness, or accepted bribes or offered them, was taught by the prophets to reflect how such conduct must look in the eyes of One whose chief passion was for justice. But this broad term of " righteousness " includes more than we include under the word "justice." It was especially the duty of a judge to protect those who were defenceless and to succour the miserable ; and so the righteousness of God included what we should more naturally speak of as His mercy. The notion, familiar in a certain type of theology, of God's righteousness and mercy as opposite, or balancing, qualities, one of which must be satisfied before the other can come into play, is altogether foreign to the teaching of the prophets. A Jew could say, " Deliver me from bloodguiltiness, O God, and my tongue shall sing of Thy righteousness." God's righteousness is the equity of perfect love, showing itself as anger against sin, but as compassion towards penitence. And yet, again, God's righteousness includes the thought of His faithfulness to the loving purpose He has for Israel, and so it is often coupled with " salvation." " There is no God else beside me, a righteous God and a Saviour." " I that speak in righteousness, mighty to save." Justice, Mercy, Salvation —these, then, are the great qualities which the prophets associate with the nature of God in His dealings with His people.

But, in the second place, they insist that God's "righteousness" must find its counterpart and reflection in the people whom He has chosen for Himself. They must be just, as He is just, merciful as He is merciful; and His "salvation" of them must be acknowledged in their "walking humbly" with Him—a correspondence which is at the very root of being able to "do justly and love mercy." This relation of the people to God is described under many names in the prophets. It is called "waiting upon God," "seeking Him," "trusting Him," "knowing Him," and it is meant to issue in the life of obedience. What is needed, therefore, is to create this conscience in the individual of a responsibility before God for His actions. We find it almost impossible to put ourselves back by imagination into a time when the religious conscience of a people was almost entirely national—that is to say, when the only evidences of God's providence were national successes and calamities, so that the ordinary well-disposed citizen did not habitually connect the thought of God's oversight with his private life. But it is clear that the prophetic teaching, though addressed to the nation as a whole, could only influence them as it influenced individuals in the nation and created this personal conscience. We cannot doubt that the writing down and circulation of the law of Deuteronomy and the writing down of the prophecies of Amos and Hosea and Isaiah helped to arouse this individual feeling of responsibility, and it was finally achieved when the nation fell, and the people in exile actually became a collection of individuals.

Then you have for the first time in Jeremiah this profound sense of the isolation of the single soul before God and the cry for a new heart.

A third truth that we owe to the prophets is the proof of the necessity of mediation, and of the qualities necessary in a mediator. The religious history of Israel is a history of great personalities raised up by God to impress upon the people the truths which He had revealed to them for that purpose. All religious truth was mediated by the prophets, but not every prophet was a mediator in the sense that he could find an entrance for his message. God put His Spirit upon the prophet —that is to say, He quickened and developed his nature to understand and sympathise with the demands of God on the one side, and the needs of man on the other; but it was not in every prophet that the perfect balance was maintained. We should not think of Elijah or Amos as a mediator; with them the revelation of the majesty of God has almost crushed out the sense of kinship with their people. But Moses, Hosea, Jeremiah—they see both sides. Moses, who saw God face to face, feels the oppression of the people in Egypt even more than they feel it themselves; and when they sin, so great is his love for them that he offers himself for destruction in their stead. Hosea passes from denunciation to pity and from pity to denunciation, as he feels in turn the childishness of the people and their ingratitude to Jehovah's love. Jeremiah, of whom we know most, is the most striking of them all for the passionateness with which he can identify

himself with both parties in the covenant;
pleading for Jehovah with the people, interceding
for the people with Jehovah; taking up the work
of a prophet against his will—for how could he
threaten the people whom he loved?—and yet
for his prophesying persecuted by the very people
of his affection. We get a hint here of what
might be accomplished by one whose human
sympathy was so perfect that he could enter into
the lives of all men, so as to understand all that
separated them from God, while his sympathy
with God was no less perfect. At the same time,
from the fact that Jeremiah was altogether despised
in his lifetime, and only after his death was taken
as the pattern of God's righteous servant suffering
for the sins of his people, we get a hint also of
what may be required even in a perfect mediator
before the hard heart of man can recognise and
confess its sin and be forgiven.

LECTURE III

So far, in investigating the gradual development among the Israelites of a knowledge of the true way of approach to God, and atonement with Him, we have met with a double method—that of the people and that of the prophets. The popular idea, surviving from the great deliverance from Egypt, which made them a nation, was that Jehovah was their own national God, whom they met to worship, as in duty bound, at sacrificial feasts, and whose favour, if famine or defeat in battle proved Him to be displeased with them, they must once more conciliate with gifts. On the other hand, the prophetic teaching was that Jehovah was dishonoured by being regarded as merely a national God, or as One who cared for sacrifices. He was the God of the whole world, who had chosen the people of Israel for His good purposes; and the one thing He required of them was "to do justly and love mercy and walk humbly with Him." As for sacrifices, they were beside the mark; they were unnecessary; and they became actually displeasing to God so far as they diverted men's minds from the one thing needful. The two

conceptions ran side by side, the people being
devoted to their customary sacrifices, and the
prophets viewing the whole ritual religion with
suspicion as a system which laid stress in the
wrong place, and with active dislike so far as
it was tainted (as it was even in Jerusalem after
Josiah's reformation) with idolatrous elements
that were actually immoral.[1]

But with the rise of Ezekiel we find a striking

---

[1] This applies, of course, only to the prophets of the eighth
century, not to Samuel and Elijah, who found no fault with
sacrifice, nor to the post-exilic prophets, like Malachi, who
laid stress upon it. Against the view taken in the text, it
has been argued that the prophets only condemn sacrifices
"defiled by wicked living, or wrong motives, or heathen
vileness, and do not attack or depreciate sacrifice in itself."
Undoubtedly they do not condemn sacrifice in itself, though
they do depreciate it ; but they place it altogether outside
the divine requirement, as a thing indifferent. I do not think
the fact can be disputed in face of such passages as the
following : "Wherewith shall I come before the Lord, and
bow myself before the high God ? Shall I come before Him
with burnt offerings, with calves of a year old ? . . . He hath
shewed thee, O man, what is good ; and what doth the Lord
require of thee, but to do justly, and to love mercy, and to
walk humbly with thy God ?" (Micah vi. 6); or again: "I
desire mercy and not sacrifice ; and the knowledge of God
more than burnt offerings ; but they are as men that have
transgressed a covenant" (Hosea vi. 6)—*i.e.* sacrifice formed
no part of God's covenant with Israel. This teaching is also
that of Jeremiah vii. 21 : " Thus saith the Lord of hosts, the
God of Israel : Add your burnt offering unto your sacrifices,
and eat ye flesh. For I spake not unto your fathers, nor
commanded them in the day that I brought them out of the
land of Egypt concerning burnt offerings or sacrifices ; but
this thing I commanded them, saying, Hearken unto my voice,
and I will be your God and ye shall be my people." And Amos
says the same thing (v. 25) : " Did ye bring unto me sacrifices

change in the prophetic attitude. Ezekiel was
a priest, who was among the first exiles taken
by Nebuchadnezzar to Babylon; and in exile
the word of the Lord came to him, and he
prophesied the complete destruction of Jerusalem
and the Temple, which came about as he foretold. But as, "in the land of the Chaldeans,
by the river Chebar," he brooded upon the
familiar worship of the ruined sanctuary—what
it had been, and what one day, by God's re-
storing power, it might be, he sketched a ritual
which should lay the main stress not on the
joyous side of religion, with its sacrificial feasts
—this was the aspect of worship still emphasised
in Deuteronomy—but on such sacrifices as were
better suited to call to mind the holiness of
God and to prepare the people for communion
with Him by sanctifying themselves. If we
turn to the prophecies of Ezekiel, we shall see
that, while in the greater part of his book he
impresses, in his own peculiar and visionary
way, the same lessons as the prophet Jeremiah,
in the last few chapters he draws a picture of a
new Jerusalem and a restored Temple, and lays

and offerings in the wilderness forty years, O house of
Israel?"

The question whether some ritual is not necessary to the
very existence of worship does not seem to have been raised
before Ezekiel. Isaiah, though he describes his own purification
as effected by a live coal from the altar (vi. 17), seems to
look forward in the future to a House of God without sacrifice
(ii. 2-4), as did Micah (iv. 1-3); at any rate it is significant
that sacrifice should not even be mentioned in this ideal
picture, as one of the purposes for which the nations should
flow to the Lord's house.

down precise rules for preserving the sanctity of everything in it—the sanctity of the buildings, of the altars, of the priests ; and puts what he calls the " law of the house " into one sentence : " The whole limit round about shall be most holy ; behold, this is the law of the house." The duty of the priests is said to be : " To teach my people the difference between the holy and the profane, and cause them to discern between the clean and the unclean." To understand the changed view of the priesthood which this sentence implies we must bear in mind how the priesthood was regarded in the law of Deuteronomy. The word " holy " has there, as in the Prophets, a moral significance, and the chief duty of the priest was still not to sacrifice, but to teach the people their duty in matters that were too difficult for them. Moreover, up to the time of Deuteronomy an Israelite could kill his own sacrifice; the only difference made by Josiah's reformation was that the high places were abolished, and their priests put on a somewhat lower level than those at Jerusalem ; but in the ideal ritual of Ezekiel no Israelite layman can kill the sacrifice ; and a further distinction is made that the priesthood is limited to the single family of Zadok, all the other priests being degraded to an inferior order, under the name of Levites. Thus there is circle beyond circle round the mercy-seat to preserve its sanctity. Holiness, in the sense of freedom from defilement, is the law of the new house.

It is not a little astonishing, when we have once realised the chasm that separates the prophetic teaching about righteousness from

6

sacrificial ceremonialism, to find it suddenly
bridged in this manner; to find a prophet laying down a scheme for securing holiness which
is so largely ceremonial. How can we explain
it? The explanation that St. Paul gave of the
whole Mosaic law applies with special force
to this ceremonial part of it—that the law came
in to supply a temporary need,[1] in order to
increase the human consciousness of sin. It was
designed to increase the sense of the distance
that separated man from God, by not allowing
him to approach the mercy-seat for himself, but
only through specially sanctified ministers. And
let us note at once that it had its intended effect
upon the restored nation. The prophets had
preached an ideal of duty to God which left
nothing to desire, but they found fault with the
traditional devotions of the people, and gave
them nothing in their place. They looked forward to a day when all the Lord's people should
be prophets; when every one, from the least
to the greatest, should hear God's word sound-
ing in his ears, and speak to Him directly in
prayer; but the mass of the people were far
below the level of the prophets. The new ritual,
as seen in vision by Ezekiel, and carried out
with modifications after the Return in Ezra's new
Temple, sought to bring home the prophetic
revelation of God's perfect righteousness, and
His requirement of righteousness from the people,
by deepening the conceptions that underlay their
customary offerings.

Its first practical object was to place an in-

[1] Rom. v. 20, παρεισῆλθεν.

surmountable barrier of division between the worship of the Jews and that of the idolaters round about them, and in this it succeeded. And it performed the same most necessary function under the tyranny of Antiochus. In the decay of political life the Levitical law was a principle of unity and organisation; it preserved, as in a hard shell, the ripening fruit of true religion.

By making all sacrifices representative of the people, offered on their behalf by appointed ministers, it did not alter the fundamental idea of sacrifice as an act of communion with God, but it laid stress on what was required to retain or recover that communion. It raised emphatically that question of the 24th Psalm, "Who shall ascend unto the hill of the Lord, and who shall rise up in His holy place?" and gave the answer, "He that hath clean hands and a pure heart." Nor, again, did it make ceremonial holiness an equivalent or substitute for moral righteousness, and so undo all the work of the prophets. For it was expressly laid down that the sacrifices were intended to remove the stain or pollution caused by careless or inadvertent wrongdoing; they were not for wilful sin; or if wilful sin had been committed, they were to remove the pollution from the community, not from the sinner. What the Levitical system certainly accomplished was to keep religion from degenerating once more into mere customary morality; it kept alive the sense of God's care; and also the sense of God's holiness. The limitations put to man's free access to the sanctuary had the effect of quickening the sense

of unworthiness; and thus a blow was aimed
not only at the careless people who were at
ease in Zion, but also at the Pharisaic spirit
which was confident in its own perfect up-
rightness.

But might it not be said that this Levitical
method of Atonement made difficult what the
prophetic method had made easy? Nothing is
so striking in the prophets as their insistence
on God's willingness to forgive, if only man
would repent. Yes; but why did the prophetic
offer fail of acceptance on any large scale? Just
because the need for repentance was not realised.
A man must have a strong sense of the holiness
of God before he can acquire any strong sense
either of his own actual unholiness or of the
holiness required of him. And it was this sense
which the sacrificial system, as developed from
the teaching of Ezekiel, was intended to foster,
and did foster. It is never hinted that God's
forgiveness is contingent upon the offering of
sacrifice. Ezekiel is prophet as well as priest;
and it is to Ezekiel that we owe that most familiar
of all the Bible texts about forgiveness: "When
the wicked man turneth away from his wickedness that he hath committed and doeth that
which is lawful and right, he shall save his soul
alive" (xviii. 27).

Let us ask now whether we can detect what
were the main ideas underlying this Levitical
ritual of atonement. It is somewhat remarkable
that the Levitical books themselves give no explanation of how the cleansing of defilement was
procured by sacrifices. The only explanation

offered is a passage in Lev. xvii. 11—" The life of the flesh is in the blood; and *I have given it you* upon the altar to make an atonement for your lives; for it is the blood that maketh atonement by means of the life." We learn from this passage that the blood is the essential part of the sacrifice because there is life in it, and it is life that makes atonement, but how or why we are not told. What is the virtue in life-blood? How can we determine? There are two possible methods. Either we may ask what were the ideas underlying sacrifice in more primitive times, or we may ask what were the leading ideas of Ezekiel, for certainly it was Ezekiel's prophecy which gave the impetus to the worship of the second Temple. The two investigations lead to very similar results.

Scholars who have investigated the history of Semitic sacrifice tell us that the importance attached to the life-blood arises from the fact that the victim originally represents the Deity, and that in primitive sacrifice it is the blood of the sacrifice that the worshippers eat so as to partake of the divine life. At a later stage the practice changes somewhat, and the worshipper, instead of feeding upon the divine flesh and blood, is thought of as sharing with God in a common meal; the blood, as the more sacred element, being poured out for the Deity, and the flesh consumed by the worshipper; but the idea of communion with the Divine Spirit as the essential idea of sacrifice remains the same; and the sense that the blood is divine is never lost, for in many forms of purification blood is sprinkled upon the worshipper or upon

the altar, just as at the Passover sacrifice it was
sprinkled on the doorposts and lintel of the
house. Why, for instance, does Ezekiel insist
that for seven days the new altar in the new
Jerusalem shall be purified by having the blood
of the sin offering cast upon it? The blood of
the sin offering, we are told, covers or cleanses
the sin; if so, that must be by virtue of its own
inherent purity. On this theory—that the blood
contains a divine life—we can understand how
it should make atonement. And remember what
happened to the rest of the sin offering after
it had been offered : it was not suffered to go
outside the temple, but was eaten by the priests
themselves in the inner court, because it was
holy (Ezek. xlvi. 20). It is clear that a theory
we sometimes meet with, that in the sin offering
the victim represents the guilty people, will not
account for these ceremonies; the sin offering
was "holy," not the reverse.

In the second place, this theory of sacrifice,
which makes God the Atoner of impurity by
virtue of His own divine life, which He once more
communicates, corresponds to the teaching that
runs all through Ezekiel. No prophet is so in-
sistent as he upon the doctrine of man's need of
regeneration, and the corresponding doctrine of
God's power and will to impart a new life. Or
the one hand, he cries, "Make you a new heart
and a new spirit, for why will ye die, O house of
Israel?" (xviii. 31); and, on the other, he brings
the promise (xxxvi. 25), "A new heart will I give
you, and a new spirit will I put within you, and
I will take away the stony heart out of your

flesh, and I will give you a heart of flesh." One
of the most impressive visions of Ezekiel is that
of the holy waters pouring from the threshold of
the house of God—a vision whose significance
has been well rendered by a modern poet :

> " East, the forefront of habitations holy
>   Gleamed to Engedi, shone to Eneglaim ;
> Softly thereout and from thereunder slowly
>   Wandered the waters, and delayed, and came.
>
> Even with so soft a surge and an increasing,
>   Drunk of the sand, and thwarted of the clod,
> Stilled, and astir, and checked, and never ceasing,
>   Spreadeth the great wave of the grace of God." [1]

The waters, as St. John expressly says in the
Revelation, are waters " of life "; even as the
blood which God gives upon the altar is blood
of life ; and both are symbols of His grace. It
is Ezekiel to whom the prophecy came—" I have
poured out my spirit upon the house of Israel,
saith the Lord God."

The sacrificial system, therefore, interpreted
according to the design of Ezekiel, would have
been a figurative representation before the eyes
of Israel of the great prophetic truths on their
religious rather than their moral side ; that God
is holy, and that, nevertheless, He vouchsafes to
dwell with His people ; that He calls them to
be holy as He is holy ; and that He will make
them holy by putting His spirit upon them.
The knowledge that day by day, morning and
evening, burnt offerings were sacrificed in the
Temple " for a sweet-smelling savour to God,"
as the phrase was—that is, as a recognition of

[1] F. Myers, *St. Paul.*

His majesty—must have helped to keep alive the sense of God's covenant promises to His people; while the inaccessibility of the mercy-seat, visited only by the high priest, and that but once a year, must have tended to keep alive the sense of the distance between them in character.

But the prophetic teaching in the decay of prophecy might never have succeeded in shining through the grossness of the sacrificial symbol but for a new development in worship. During the Exile, when sacrifice was impossible, the custom grew up of meeting together for mutual encouragement and common devotion, and this habit must have quickened the power of prayer among the faithful, just as the new custom of writing down the divine law and publishing prophecies must have quickened the power of meditation on God's Word. The synagogue service, therefore, which continued everywhere after the Return, must have increased the spirituality of Jewish worship, by supplying regular opportunity for that personal and direct communion with God in penitence and prayer and praise which is necessary to the very existence of spiritual religion, and is of the essence of the prophetic commandment—" Thou shalt love the Lord thy God with all thy heart, and with all thy soul, and with all thy mind." How the sacrifices were regarded by devout souls both before and after the Exile we have most interesting evidence in the Book of Psalms. In some Psalms, such as the 4th and 20th and 118th, sacrifice is regarded as the normal expression of worship; whereas in others the sacrifices are either put on one side, in the spirit of the early prophets, as things that may divert the mind from the one thing needful, or else interpreted in terms of human devotion. Thus in Psalm xl. we read—"Sacrifice and offering thou hast no delight in; burnt offering and sin offering thou hast not required; but mine ears hast thou opened. Then said I, Lo, I am come: in the roll of the book [my duty] is prescribed to me [Deut. vi. 6]; I delight to do thy will, O my God; yea, thy law is within my heart." This is the prophetic doctrine, pure and simple—"To obey is better than sacrifice." In Psalm l., however, the sacrifices are not altogether put aside in favour of obedience—they are allegorised. God speaks to the Jews as to those with whom He "has made a covenant with sacrifice"; but the covenant sacrifice is interpreted to mean "thanksgiving and prayer." "Thinkest thou that I will eat bull's flesh or drink the blood of goats? Sacrifice unto God thanksgiving; and call upon me in the day of trouble." This is in the spirit of that unique phrase of Hosea (xiv. 2), "we will offer the calves of our lips." In Psalm li., again, the alternative to sacrifice, or its true meaning, is declared to be penitence—"Thou delightest not in sacrifice, else would I give it; thou hast no pleasure in burnt offering; the sacrifices of God are a broken spirit, a broken and contrite heart, O God, thou wilt not despise." It thus came about that, without allegorising each particular kind of sacrifice, and saying that one represented "obedience" and another "thanks-

7

giving," and another " penitence " (which would
not have answered to the facts, for the same
sort of sacrifice was offered with different in-
tentions), the better spirits among the nation,
although they may have differed as to whether
sacrifices were ordained in the original covenant,
came in practice to regard them as an acted
language in which, at the national shrine, and on
public occasions, the sentiments of piety for which
God looked—obedience, prayer, penitence—were
represented before Him symbolically, and God
gave through His appointed ministers an answer
of peace.

In order, therefore, to ascertain the post-exilic
teaching about Atonement it is unnecessary, even
if it were possible, to attempt a *rationale* of the
sacrifices ; it is simpler and more satisfactory
to examine the point of view of the later
Psalms. We have seen that the doctrine of
God's free forgiveness following upon the sinner's
repentance was proclaimed by all the prophets ;
that truth shines through all the Psalms, and is
never lost. Take, for example, Psalm xxxii.,
" Blessed is the man whose unrighteousness is
forgiven." Whatever difficulty there was in
bringing the sin home to the psalmist's conscience,
he recognises that the whole transaction as
between himself and God is on his side confession
and on God's pardon : " I said I will confess my
transgressions unto the Lord, and thou forgavest
the iniquity of my sin." The difficult matter
continues to be the creation of this sensitive
conscience. We have already seen that one
cause that helped towards the development of

conscience was the symbolism of the sacrifices
of Atonement. Another was the watchful habit
of mind that was due to the circulation of the
codes of law, first the Deuteronomic and then
the Levitical. And a third was the constant
affliction that was the lot of the people for many
generations.

It has been said by some that the influence of
the written law was rather to beget a sense of
righteousness than a sense of sin. Such late
Psalms as the 1st and 119th, while they breathe
a delight in the law, have yet little to say about
confession of sin, and we may admit that Phari-
saism may lie further down the path along which
they conduct the worshipper. But in themselves
they are not Pharisaic, and they contain verses
which give evidence of that reflective temper
which brings self-knowledge. " Moreover, by
them is thy servant warned." " I am thy servant,
give me understanding, that I may keep thy
statutes." And, not to multiply examples, it is
clear that the writer of the 139th Psalm, " O
Lord, thou hast searched me out," must have
been in the habit of squaring his conduct by the
rule of the divine law : " Try me, O God, and know
my heart, prove me and examine my thought,
look well if there be any way of wickedness in
me, and lead me in the way everlasting."

A further influence lay in the experience of
suffering. It has been well said by a distinguished
Jewish writer that "at his worst the individual
Israelite felt that he belonged to the people of
God, and shared their righteousness ; and at his
best he still felt the depressing burden of Israel's

national sins."[1] This latter feeling came to him through the national afflictions. We see this, for example, in Psalm cxliii. 2, " Enter not into judgment with thy servant, for in thy sight shall no man living be righteous : for the enemy hath persecuted my soul." It is the persecution that has pricked the conscience. The connection of sin with sorrow was deep-ingrained in the Jewish people. But so strong was the sense of national unity that the possibility was recognised that the sin might be committed by one part of the nation and the suffering borne by another. As the Psalms give utterance, for the most part, to the sentiments of the Jewish Church as a whole, this thought could hardly come to clear expression in them, though in one or two, notably the 22nd, where the sufferings are understood to be the sufferings of the righteous, it is made plain that they are in some way to have a redemptive influence upon others. But in a prophecy, the date of which is still disputed, referring to the Servant of Jehovah, the doctrine of vicarious suffering is laid down in unambiguous terms, and with a force and beauty which have made it perhaps the best-known and best-loved passage in the Old Testament. This Servant of God, who in the first reference may stand (as other descriptions in preceding chapters seem to show) for the ideal Israel, has been afflicted, and judged, and executed ; and at first those who look on imagine that he is suffering for his own sins. But presently it is borne in upon them that the Servant is suffering not for his sins, but for

[1] Montefiore, *Hibbert Lectures.*

theirs. And the prophet, by a bold metaphor taken from the ritual which is perhaps without a parallel in the prophetic literature, declares that the Servant is made a sin offering, whose blood may cleanse their pollution. By which piece of symbolism he means, as he distinctly says, that it was in the will and purpose of God that the sufferings of the innocent should be used for the conversion of the guilty, as they came to reflect upon them. "Surely he hath borne our griefs and carried our sorrows; yet we did esteem him smitten of God and afflicted. But he was wounded for our trangressions, he was bruised for our iniquities." That is their first conviction. Then it is seen that this must be the Lord's doing. "It pleased the Lord to bruise him." And then the purpose in God's providence is seen to be what it actually was—their own conversion: "Thy righteous servant shall make many righteous, and bear the burden of their iniquities."

One further thought of the Psalter remains to be noticed, a thought of the highest importance to the doctrine of Atonement: that as God in His love gives commandments and looks for obedience, and in His love may send suffering (upon whom He will within the community, for we are all members one of another) to arouse a sense of disobedience, so neither penitence nor newness of life is possible without the influence of the Spirit vouchsafed by the same love of God. This lesson, hinted at in the earlier prophets (Hosea xiv. 2; Micah vii. 19), but first clearly taught by Jeremiah and Ezekiel, receives its

classical expression in the words of Psalm li.:
"Create in me a clean heart, O God, and renew
a right spirit within me. Cast me not away
from thy presence, and take not thy holy spirit
from me."

LECTURE IV

WE approach at last the very centre of our subject as we proceed to inquire what we can gather from the Evangelists as to our Lord's own teaching about the Atonement between God and man which He came to accomplish. But before we do so it will be well shortly to resume the doctrine as we have found it taught in the Old Testament by the prophets. It comprises a doctrine about God, a doctrine about man, and a doctrine about the means of communion between them. The doctrine about God is that He is the Creator of man, a God whose nature is righteousness and love; the doctrine about man is that he is meant to become like God, living among his fellows a life of righteousness and love, and that if he is unrighteous and unloving he sins against God; the doctrine of communion is that God desires that man should know and love Him, "with all his heart, and mind, and soul, and strength," for by the knowledge and love of God he will understand God's will, and do it. What interferes with this consummation, therefore, is defect of knowledge and defect of love; and so any process of atonement must be twofold : a revelation of God's nature, and a change of man's disposition towards Him.   Atonement is consequently a divine task ; God alone can reveal Himself to man, and God alone can change man's heart; and the history of the Jewish people is, from our point of view, a history of God's gracious work of redemption in these two ways—the work of revealing His own mind and will, and the work of creating in man a conscience to receive and respond to the revelation.   This redeeming work He committed to mediators—Moses and the succeeding prophets—whose function, therefore, was the double one of bringing to men the knowledge of God's love and righteousness, and opening men's hearts so far as they could to welcome it, in order that they might surrender whatever separated them from the will of God.   When prophecy closes it has been made clear that, although God does not compel man's will, yet redemption, not only as revelation, but as the acceptance of revelation, is of God's grace; that God must give not only the knowledge of His will in commandments, but also the power to obey them.   And the last word of Old Testament prophecy is the doctrine of God's Spirit as not only dictating a law from outside, but as writing it on man's own heart, and giving him power to fulfil it.   And so the prayer goes up : " With thee is the fountain of life," " Stablish me with thy free spirit."

In strange contrast with this prophetic doctrine of God's grace as a fountain of living waters was the teaching of the Pharisees in our Lord's day. It had long been recognised through the teaching of the prophets, and the impression left upon the minds of the nation by the system of Levitical sacrifices, that the one thing that separated between man and God was sin; but to the further question, how this separating sin was to be removed, the Pharisees had given an answer which was not the answer of the prophets. The idea which had been inherited from Isaiah of a kingdom of God upon earth was understood to presuppose a righteous people. Messiah could not come and restore the kingdom to Israel until the people were worthy of it—that is to say, until they were thoroughly obedient to the law of God; and, consequently, the effort was made by the Pharisees to apply to the law a principle akin to that adopted in the Levitical system—of preserving the holiness of a central shrine by a system of barricades built round it. Just as the "Holy of Holies" within the Temple was surrounded by a series of courts, so each commandment was hedged about by a double and treble fence of subsidiary commandments, in order that, if these traditions were kept, it might be impossible to profane the central commandment itself. On this system, therefore, each man must save himself from sin; and those who would not take the trouble to do so must be excommunicated. God's part would begin when the whole nation, or the faithful remnant, had achieved its own righteousness.

The Gospels, however, make it evident that there were still pious souls whose view of the share God must take in the salvation of His

8

people was very different from this.   In the song
of Zechariah (the father of John Baptist) it is
said of the future prophet: "Thou shalt go
before the face of God, to prepare his ways, to
give knowledge of the salvation of his people
[which is to consist] in the remission of their
sins."   And, accordingly, in order that the remission may take effect, John summons the people
to repent, and he repeats the prophetic promise
that God will send One who shall baptize
"the people with his holy spirit" (Isa. xliv. 3,
Joel ii. 28, Ezek. xxxvi. 27).   John, therefore, is
in line with the prophets, and our Lord, when
He begins His ministry, places Himself in line
with John and with the ancient prophets, whom
He quotes continually, as against the Pharisees.
At the bottom of the antagonism between our
Lord and the Pharisees lies this fundamental
difference as to the part God and man must play
in the redemption of the people.   The Pharisee,
in our Lord's parable, who goes up to the Temple
to pray, is, in fact, reminding God that he, at
least, is ready for the Messianic kingdom, because
not only had he kept the bare letter of the law,
but had done many works of supererogation.
He asks for nothing.   The Gospel of Jesus, on
the other hand, was summed up in His very
name : God is salvation.   " He shall save his
people."   When the Pharisees looked askance
at Him for mixing with the excommunicate, He
replied, in terms of which they would not have
recognised either the irony or the religion,
" They that are whole do not need the physician ;
I came not to call the righteous, but sinners."

Our Lord then came as the Saviour. In His
first discourse in the synagogue of Nazareth
He bases His mission on the great promise in
Isaiah lxi. 1 : " The Spirit of the Lord God is
upon me, because he hath anointed me to heal,
to bind up, to deliver "—in a word, to save.
In a public miracle of healing at Capernaum
he takes occasion to make clear that the healing
of the body is but an outward sign of the power
to heal the spirit—" He saith unto the sick of
the palsy, Son, be of good cheer, thy sins be
forgiven thee " (Matt. ix. 2).

We may go on, therefore, to inquire in what,
according to our Lord's teaching, this forgiveness
of sins consisted. In the story of the paralytic
mention is made of one condition, that of " faith."
The paralytic was attracted to Jesus ; he believed
that Jesus could exercise the great power of
God ; and the opening of this channel of faith,·
whereby the power of God (which is the love
of God) could flow into his nature, was the
condition, and, so far as the story shows, the
only condition, necessary for forgiveness. The
forgiveness was an act of Divine grace, and,
at the same time, of Divine faith, recognising
and fostering the seeds of future righteousness ;
blowing into flame the smoking flax by the
breath of the Holy Spirit. The story of the
woman who was a sinner dwells emphatically
upon personal attraction to Christ as the dis-
posing cause of repentance. She came into the
house where He was, and washed His feet with
her tears ; and the response came, " Her sins,
which were many, are forgiven, because she

loved much" (St. Luke vii. 47). The attraction
to Christ, expressed in one case by faith, in the
other by love, was (as it were) the opening of
the heart through which the power of God could
enter to heal the soul. We see the same attraction at work in the case of Zacchæus. If we ask
wherein lay the peculiar attractiveness that drew
these sinners, must we not reply that it was the
divine compassion—the holiness and the love—
that lit up the face of Jesus Christ? Our Lord
drew the sinners to Him by the revelation
He brought them through His presence of the
Fatherly love of God. The influence of His
Spirit upon their spirits proved Him to be the
true Mediator. To understand the love and
righteousness of the Father, as Christ displayed
it, was necessarily to be drawn into sonship. A
new impulse Godward was implanted in the old
nature, which would draw the energies into
itself and so lead to a new life. What this
new life of sonship must consist in—what love
to God and man—and how it must differ from
what passed for righteousness in the religious
estimation of the time, our Lord taught on many
occasions and by many parables; but we need
not consider it now in any detail. One principle
is important for our present purpose. Our Lord
gave His sanction to the doctrine of the prophets
as to God's constant love of all men, evil as well
as good, and His readiness to forgive whenever
they would look to Him in penitence; and He
taught most emphatically that if men would be
children of the Father in heaven, they too must
bear in their hearts always this great love and

this readiness to forgive. Mercifulness was to be not the least sign that they were of the divine family, for they were to plead it when they approached the Father in prayer : " Forgive us our sins; we forgive those who sin against us." The divine and human forgiveness are again and again drawn into a parallel; the one is to be as free and full and constant as the other. In each case the forgiveness cannot take effect unless he who has done the wrong will admit it and repent. But on the side of the wronged one there can be no other condition.

The readiness of the infinite love of God to forgive, in contrast with the unreadiness even of religious men, was taught by our Lord in a parable which has carried conviction to men's hearts from the first age till now, and will continue to do so as long as the Gospels are read—the parable of the Prodigal Son. No single parable can teach more than a portion of the truth; and this parable says nothing of the father's care for his disobedient son while he was in the far country or of messages sent to bring him back; but on the points of which it speaks it must be understood to speak the very mind of Christ. And the truth of all truths which it enshrines for ever is that of the un-restrained and unconditioned forgiveness that the Father vouchsafes to the children who come back to Him confessing their unworthiness, and the new life He gives them in His presence. If, then, the question is asked, What exactly did Christ mean by the forgiveness of sins ? this parable supplies the answer. Christian forgiveness is the recognition by love of a change of mind in the sinner; it is impossible except to love; and it has its perfect work when it calls out love in return.

We learn, then, from the Gospels what was Christ's mediatorial way of salvation. He saved men by attracting them to Himself, and so showing them the Father; by forgiving them their sins; and by giving them, through the channel of their faith and love to Him, the power of His Spirit to enable them for a new life. It was all "of grace." And these facts of salvation correspond to the theory of salvation, if we may call it so, which is laid down in St. John's Gospel (iii. 16), "God so loved the world that he gave his only begotten Son, that whosoever believeth in him should not perish but have eternal life." The world was perishing because, not knowing God, it missed the true Fountain of Life; but to know God was inevitably to love Him and grow into His likeness; and to believe in Christ was the God-appointed way to know God. With this doctrine of St. John agrees that parable of the Husbandmen, which tells how the owner of the vineyard sends his only son to remind those who had forgotten him of their obligations. He sent messengers not a few, and at last, having one only son, well-beloved, he sent him; for he said, "My son they will reverence" (Mark xii. 6).

But, as we know, they killed him and cast him out of the vineyard. And so we must go on to inquire, if God's good purpose in sending His Son to win us to Himself by the revelation of His love was frustrated by the guardians of

His own vineyard, how their malice was over-ruled; for out of the apparent triumph of evil God has ever worked its overthrow.

But first it may be necessary to clear definitely out of the way an idea sometimes met with in popular theology, that our Lord's death was commanded by the Father Himself; and that our Lord, in obedience to this commandment, came to die. The saying just quoted from the parable of the Husbandmen, "They will reverence my son," is sufficient of itself to make such a motive for the Incarnation impossible, for the motive which that saying supplies—and it is our Lord Himself who speaks the parable—is inconsistent with it. The only passage in the Gospels that even superficially lends countenance to such an idea is a text in St. John (x. 17): "Therefore doth my Father love me, because I lay down my life that I may take it again. No man taketh it away from me, but I lay it down of myself. I have power to lay it down and I have power to take it again. This commandment have I received of my Father." To understand this passage it must be observed that it refers to the parable of the Good Shepherd which precedes it. The Good Shepherd has been placed by commandment of the Father in charge of His sheep; and a wolf (called in xiv. 30 the Prince of the World) has attacked him. A hireling might be tempted to save his life, by deserting the sheep and fleeing. The Good Shepherd will rather lay down His life, perceiving that to give His life for the sheep falls within the commandment of God, who has given Him charge over them. The commandment of God refers, therefore, primarily to the care of the sheep. And this interpretation is supported by the prayer recorded in the seventeenth chapter, which though offered by our Lord in immediate expectation of death, contains no reference to that death as being undergone by the commandment of the Father. The only commandment there spoken of is the work of revealing the Father's nature : "*I have glorified thee on the earth,* I have finished the work which thou gavest me to do."[1] The agony in Gethsemane with the prayer that the "cup" of the crucifixion might "pass" becomes unintelligible, if to drink that cup was not the unavoidable consequence of the Incarnation, but its recognised purpose.

We may now proceed to examine the passages in which our Lord spoke to His disciples about His death. He had foreseen the event even before the open hostility of the Pharisees drove Him from the synagogues. When He was asked, at the beginning of His ministry, why His disciples did not fast, He replied, "Can the children of the bridechamber fast as long as the bridegroom is with them ? But," He added, "the days will come when the bridegroom shall be taken away from them, and

[1] For those who do not read Greek it may be added that St. Paul's phrase (Phil. ii. 8) "became obedient *unto* death" does not mean "obedient to the command to die," but "obedient even though the result of obedience was death"; the preposition being the same as in the phrase (Heb. xii. 4) "Ye have not resisted *unto* blood," *i.e.* "resisted though the result should be martyrdom."

then shall they fast in those days." It was not, however, till the faith of the disciples had strengthened into the confession of His Messiah- ship at Cæsarea Philippi, that He began to prepare them for His death. And then the announcement is explicit: " He began to teach them, that the Son of man must suffer many things, and be rejected by the elders, and the chief priests, and the scribes, and be killed" (Mark viii. 31). The announcement is repeated after the Transfiguration as they went through Galilee: " He taught his disciples, and said unto them, The Son of man is delivered up into the hands of men, and they shall kill him" (ix. 31); and again, as they approached Jeru- salem : " He took again the twelve, and began to tell them the things that were going to happen unto him, saying, Behold, we go up to Jeru- salem ; and the Son of man shall be delivered unto the chief priests and the scribes, and they shall condemn him to death" (x. 32, 33). Our Lord's prevision of His coming death was, to some extent, what we can explain by ordinary insight and foresight. Attempts had already been made to kill Him, and such attempts must at last be successful. But still more He bases His conviction on what had happened to the old prophets. " No prophet can perish out of Jerusalem "—*i.e.*, there is an inevitable antagonism between an organised ecclesiastical system and a new revelation from God. Jerusalem, the city of God, is also the slayer of the prophets of God. The keepers of God's vineyard will do to the Son what they have done already to the servants.

9

But this conviction of His approaching death carried with it, to our Lord's mind, more than the bare fact, and more even than the certainty of the Resurrection that lay beyond it. It carried with it also a comprehension of the part it was to play in the accomplishment of His own purpose, which was the salvation of men. There is a whole series of passages in the Gospels which lay stress upon its necessity; and our object must be to try and comprehend our Lord's meaning in speaking thus of His death as necessary. For example, speaking of the Son of Man coming in His kingdom, He says (Luke xvii. 22): "But first must he suffer many things, and be rejected of this generation." How are we to interpret this "must"? The answer seems given by a verse that follows in the next chapter (xviii. 31): "Behold, we go up to Jerusalem, and all the things that are written by the prophets shall be accomplished unto the Son of man." And again, at the moment of betrayal, "The Son of man indeed goeth, as it is written of him" (Mark xiv. 21); and after the Resurrection, on the journey to Emmaus, the doctrine is laid down that the Christ must have suffered, and, through suffering, enter into His glory, according to the teaching of Moses and all the prophets. In none of these places are the particular words of the prophets referred to, and we shall learn nothing from mere conjecture as to what were the prophetic sayings which our Lord had in mind. Happily in one passage there is a direct quotation. In St. Luke xxii. 37 we read, "I say unto you, that this which is written must be fulfilled in me,

And he was reckoned with transgressors; for that which concerneth me hath fulfilment." The quotation here is from the fifty-third chapter of Isaiah, and to understand our Lord's reference we must bear in mind the meaning of that ancient prophecy which we were considering in the last lecture. The subject of the prophecy is the redemptive power of suffering. Speculation turned, as it could not fail to turn, during the Exile upon the reason why the innocent and God-fearing members of the Jewish people should be involved in the calamity which they recognised to be due to the sins of the nation. Was not God confusing innocent with guilty? Isaiah's answer is No. In the sufferings of the righteous there is saving virtue. The truth may have been brought home to him by the sufferings of some particular prophet, such as Jeremiah, accepted without murmuring and without ceasing from his work of proclaiming the truth—sufferings which had visibly brought many to repentance as they reflected upon them; but however this may have been, the prophet was inspired to lay down the doctrine that no way to produce conviction of heart was so sure as that of suffering for the truth, and he was inspired to declare that this was God's foreordained plan to bring men to repentance. The servant of God must not strive; he is to win his success by gentleness, not by force; he will not resent, much less retaliate. Why? Because patience under oppression makes the oppressors consider; they recognise that such humility is more than human, and in proportion as they acknowledge

the divine support given to the sufferer, they
must acknowledge his goodness and their own
blindness; so their eyes are opened to see the
truth; by the stripes they themselves have in-
flicted they are themselves healed.   And this,
says the prophet, is no accident, but a divine
means for the redemption of men.   The Lamb of
God is led to the slaughter; and lo! the
slaughter-house turns out to be the very altar
of sacrifice, and the murderers are pouring out
the blood which may avail to cleanse their own
pollution.

This was the prophecy which our Lord applied
to Himself.   "He was numbered with transgressors" in order that He might take away the
iniquities of those who were indeed transgressors,
by producing compunction of heart.   He died—
in His own words—"that the world may know
that I love the Father, and as the Father gave
me commandment, even so I do."   And when the
thief on the cross, seeing His patience, said,
"This man hath done nothing amiss; Jesus, remember me when thou comest in thy kingdom,"
the prophecy began to be fulfilled; our Lord
began, even before His death, to see of the
travail of His soul.   This view of an atoning
efficacy in our Lord's death—that it drew man
to God in penitence—is also that of the famous
comparison in St. John to the brazen serpent
lifted up for the children of Israel to see (iii. 14);
a saying which is further explained by that
other: "When ye have lifted up the Son of
man, then ye shall know that I am he" (viii. 28);
and by the world-wide vision that followed the

desire of the Greeks to see Him : "I, if I be lifted up from the earth, will draw all men unto me" (xii. 32). The world will look, and comprehend, and repent, and love.

And this helps us to understand why our Lord brings the thought of His death into direct connection with the fact that He was Messiah, the King. The cross will be the throne of the world. His first clear announcement of His death followed immediately upon St. Peter's confession of the kingship ; a second followed the request of James and John for the position of viceroys in the kingdom. To them our Lord replied, in effect, You want to reign ; but can you suffer ? In My kingdom, power over men is proportioned to what you can do for them in the way of service ; and service means suffering. "If any one will come after me, let him take up his cross." "The Son of man came not to be served, but to serve, and to give his life a ransom for many." The general sense of this passage is clear ; it implies that the true king of men—that is, the king who exercises real sway over men's hearts—is he who lives his life entirely in their interests, who spends his strength for them. The true king is a shepherd who exists for the sake of his flock and will lay down his life, if need be, in their defence. But what is the particular force of the words " to give his life a ransom for many "? The question was raised by later theology as to whether the ransom was paid to the devil or to God ; the one answer being as impossible as the other. That the question should have been debated at all is an example of the power words have to "shoot back upon the understanding." We, at any rate, may remember that we still speak of delivering some one at great "cost" to ourselves without implying that the expense of our spirit is paid over to any one else. Many attempts, also, have been made to guess at the particular image that was in our Lord's mind. But guesses with nothing to guide us cannot be convincing. We are on safer ground in reminding ourselves what would have happened if our Lord had played the hireling shepherd and preferred His own safety to the deliverance of the flock. In that case He would not have offended the Pharisees, which means He must have accepted their ideas of God and righteousness and duty, and their ideas of the Kingdom. The sinners would not have been called to forgiveness. There would have been no parable of the Prodigal Son or of the repentant Publican, no Sermon on the Mount, no comfortable words to the weary and heavy-laden. Good men would have been still in the Pharisaic or some other prison. But at the very outset of His mission He had rejected the policy of compromise as a temptation of the devil. And so the price of our freedom was the life of our King. He proved His kingship by paying it. He gave his life a ransom for many. And as a result His kingdom is an everlasting kingdom. The world has gone after Him. This is, at any rate, the explanation of Christ's words that approved itself to St. Peter: "Ye were not redeemed," he says, "by corruptible things, as silver and gold, *from your vain way of life received by tradition from your fathers* [that was the prison in which we were bound]; but you were redeemed with the precious blood of Christ."

In these two aspects of His death, as convincing men of sin, and attracting them to the Kingdom, our Lord does not refer to it as unique, for He invites His disciples to take up their cross and follow Him. There will be thrones in His kingdom for those who drink of His cup and are baptized with His baptism; and always and everywhere the blood of the martyrs is the seed of the Church. But there is one other great word of Christ which sets His death before us in an aspect in which it has no fellow. It comes in the story of the Last Supper, which is thus told by St. Mark: "And as they were eating, he took bread, and when he had blessed, he brake it, and gave to them, and said, Take ye: this is my body. And he took a cup, and when he had given thanks, he gave to them: and they drank of it. And he said unto them, This is my blood of the [new] covenant, which is shed for many;" St. Matthew adds, "for remission of sins." The first thing to note about this passage is that in it our Lord announces the fulfilment of a prophecy of Jeremiah (xxxi. 31), "Behold, the days come, saith Jehovah, that I will make a new covenant with the house of Israel and the house of Judah: not according to the covenant that I made with their fathers in the day that I took them by the hand to bring them out of the land of Egypt; which my covenant they brake, although I was an husband unto them, saith Jehovah. But this is the covenant that I will

make with the house of Israel after those days:
I will put my law into their inward parts,
and in their heart will I write it; and I will
be their God, and they shall be my people:
and they shall teach no more every man
his neighbour, and every man his brother,
saying, Know Jehovah; for they shall all know
me, from the least of them unto the greatest
of them, saith Jehovah, for I will forgive
their iniquity, and their sin I will remember no
more." The promise here is not only to forgive
past sin, but to make it impossible to sin in the
future by writing the law on the very heart,
or, as Ezekiel says, by giving a "new" heart, a
new spirit of life. Our Lord had already given
instruction on this new life in the discourses, recorded by St. John, about the Bread of Life and the
Mission of the Comforter. In fulfilment of Isaiah's
prophecy, "They shall all be taught of God,"[1]
He had come from the Father that those who
believed on Him might have eternal life. By
believing on Him they received into their hearts
a new life, which was indeed Christ Himself.
They ate His flesh and drank His blood. With
that discourse in our mind, we can be at no
loss to interpret the words used at the Last
Supper, "Take, eat, this is my body; drink ye
all of this, for this is my blood." Christ, because
He is leaving them, is bequeathing to them, as
a new spirit of life,—a spirit which is proved
to be a spirit of love unto death,—His very
self; slain, yet ever-living.

We have, then, in this last saying of our Lord

[1] liv. 13 ; John vi. 45.

a deeper revelation than those which preceded it. Always and everywhere it is true that the sufferings and death of the righteous, cheerfully accepted as a part of their service to God and man, do in God's providence set free their spirit to work in men's hearts:

> "They come apparelled in more precious habit,
> *More* moving-delicate, and *full of life*
> Than when they 'lived' indeed."

This is a principle of the divine government. From the stoning of Stephen issues, by direct spiritual consequence, the conversion of Saul. But though there are many servants, there is but one Son in whom the Father is well pleased. And the sending of *His* Spirit into the hearts of men, inasmuch as it is the Spirit of God, could mean nothing less than the redemption of the world. Thus the Atonement depends upon the Incarnation. We cannot doubt there was in our Lord's thought, as He spoke the solemn words of institution at the first Eucharist, not only Jeremiah's prophecy of the new Covenant, but the story of the sacrifice at the inauguration of the old Covenant at Mount Sinai (Exod. xxiv. 8), in which the blood of the victim, as representing the Divine life, was sprinkled both upon the altar and upon the worshippers, to bind God and man in one. That covenant sacrifice was only a symbol; and until God was revealed as very Love, who would not shrink even from death to bless His creatures, it must have been also an imperfectly apprehended symbol—for the death of the victim would have no significance except as a means of releasing the life-blood. But if Christ, by carrying His love for mankind to its final consummation in death, could pour out upon mankind His own very Spirit of love, which was nothing less than the very Spirit of God, would not this bind God and man together in an indissoluble covenant, within the unity of the Divine Spirit ? That, indeed, is the Atonement. And the Gospel now, as when Christ first preached it, is a Gospel of God's free pardon to all who will allow themselves to be drawn within the operation of the Spirit of Christ, that He may lift their hearts in love to the Father, and draw them after Him along the road of obedience to the Father's will.

LECTURE V

THE DOCTRINE OF ST. PAUL'S EPISTLES

WE saw in the last lecture that the chief and all-important difference between our Lord's doctrine of righteousness and that of the Pharisees was that our Lord brought a gospel of God's free pardon to penitence and God's free Spirit to enable men to live a new life after God's will; whereas the Pharisees trusted in themselves that they had already attained righteousness by their own precaution and zeal. We should expect, therefore, when we take up the writings of a converted Pharisee to find this contrast running through them. We should expect the keynote of his teaching to be, "By grace are ye saved; not of yourselves; it is the gift of God"; and so we find it. St. Paul's gospel is before all else a gospel of grace. The texts that rise to memory as especially characteristic of St. Paul are such as these: "Where sin abounded grace did much more abound;" "We are not under law, but under grace;" "The forgiveness of our trespasses according to the riches of his grace;" "By the grace of God I am what I am;" and his constant prayer for all his converts is that "the grace of the Lord Jesus Christ" may always be with them.

That this doctrine of grace is fundamental with St. Paul we are shown in the clearest manner by the story of what his conversion really meant to him, as it is told us by himself from the inside in the seventh chapter of his letter to the Romans. His attempt to secure his own righteousness broke down at the Tenth commandment, "Thou shalt not covet"—a commandment which carries obedience from outward action to inward impulse. However he might abstain from evil deeds, he found himself without control of evil desire. And more than so: he tells us that evil desires multiplied in proportion as he laboured to keep them in check, so that his own effort to keep the commandment resulted only in more persistent breaking of it. The fault, he tells us, was not in his mind or will: "I delight in the law of God after the inward man; but I see a different law in my members warring against the law of my mind, and bringing me into captivity under the law of sin which is in my members" (Rom. vii. 22).

Righteousness, therefore, it is all too plain, cannot be won by a man's own unaided effort, because the flesh itself is sinful; it desires endlessly, and it desires what is against the law of God. There are two principles, says St. Paul, within myself, and they are at war; with the mind I serve the law of God, but with the flesh the law of sin; and that war must go on, so far as I am concerned, for ever. I cannot deliver myself, for both combatants are myself. And so he cries: "O wretched man that I am; who shall deliver me out of the body of this death?" And then he gives the answer that his conversion brought him : "I thank God through Jesus Christ our Lord." To St. Paul Jesus Christ had proved Himself the strong Deliverer who released the "mind of the spirit" in him from slavery to the "mind of the flesh" by reinforcing the former and slaying the latter; and this He accomplished by flooding his nature with the Divine Spirit. It is evident, then, that when St. Paul speaks of salvation by grace he means salvation by the gift to man of Christ's own nature. The grace of our Lord Jesus Christ, as it is the love of God, so also it is the communication to men of the Holy Spirit. As he says emphatically to the Corinthians, "The Lord is the Spirit" (2 Cor. iii. 17). And St. Paul is simply following his Master in finding both the only possibility and the real fact of Atonement in the presence in man's heart of the Spirit of Christ and of God. Our Lord had expressed the perfect unity of Himself and the Father with believers in two phrases : first, "That they may be one in us"; and then, "I in them and thou in me." And St. Paul has the same two complementary expressions; he says both that Christ is in the Christian, and that the Christian is in Christ, the latter expression being used for the most part when he is laying down the doctrine of the union of all believers in Christ's mystical Body. Passages will readily occur to the memory where the essence of the Atonement is placed in the gift of the Spirit. The Second Man is the Lord from heaven, who is *life-giving* Spirit (1 Cor. xv. 45, 47). No man can say, "Jesus is Lord," or, indeed, "Abba, Father," "but in the

Holy Spirit " (1 Cor. xii. 3 ; Gal. iv. 6). Christians are formally addressed as "sanctified in Jesus Christ" (1 Cor. i. 2); they are "spiritual" (Gal. vi. 1 ; 1 Cor. ii. 15, etc.); they are "a temple of God," inasmuch as the Spirit of God dwelleth in them (1 Cor. iii. 16); "they are washed, sanctified, and justified in the Spirit of our God" (vi. 11); and this Divine Spirit shed abroad in our hearts manifests itself not only in astonishing signs, such as speaking with tongues and prophesying, but in faith, hope, and love, and many other "fruits of the Spirit."

But, it may be asked, Does not St. Paul lay the main stress in his doctrine of the Atonement not upon "grace," but upon "faith"? Does he not expressly say, "Being justified *by faith* we have peace with God through our Lord Jesus Christ, by whom also we have access [*by faith*] into this grace wherein we stand"?—putting faith before grace as a necessary pre-condition of its reception. And the answer is, "Certainly he does"; just as our Lord does Himself. Since God created man in His own image, man's will cannot be forced; and so we find that our Lord could not heal in body or soul any but those who came to Him in faith. Still, there can be no doubt which of the two necessary factors is in St. Paul's judgment the more vital. He lays stress on faith, not in opposition to grace, but in opposition to the works of the law. That is to say, he is minimising the human element in Atonement, not magnifying it. As a Pharisee he had held that a man was made righteous before God by perfect obedience to the divine

law ; this obedience he had in his own experience
found to be impossible, because he could not
control desire, and he found that evil desire was
killed only by the new grace which he received
by accepting Jesus Christ as his Lord.   The
acceptance was a necessary condition of the peace
with God, but it was not the cause of it—" We
have peace with God through our Lord Jesus
Christ," though we have " access by faith unto
grace."   And still more, St. Paul was conscious
that even man's faith was only possible through
divine grace ; and in its developed form as love
of Christ was one of the choicest fruits of the
Divine Spirit (1 Cor. xiii. 13).   So that the perfect
communion in which the Christian life consists
may be described as a life of faith or as a life
of grace, according as it is looked at from below
or from above ; and it is interesting to find St.
Paul himself describing it in these two ways in
the same passage (Gal. ii. 20): first he says,
' Christ liveth in me " ; and then, without a pause,
he goes on, " The life which I now live in the
flesh I live by faith in the Son of God."

So far, then, the teaching of St. Paul about
the Atonement corresponds closely with that of
our Lord Himself, as we find it recorded in the
Gospels.   We may now go on to inquire in what
way St. Paul considers our Lord's death to have
ministered to the Atonement ; and our first question must be, Does he lay stress, as our Lord
Himself does, on the sacrificial aspects of the
death, both as manifesting His obedience to the
Father and as a means of conveying His life of
obedience to others ?   The prevalence of this

doctrine among the first preachers of Christianity is obscured in the Authorised Version by the failure to recognise in the word παῖς the Servant of God, of whom Isaiah prophesied—*e.g.*, in Acts iii. 26, "God having raised up his *Servant* [A.V. Son] Jesus, sent him to bless you, in turning away every one of you from your iniquities." This is the doctrine which forms the staple of the "preaching of Jesus" given by Philip to the eunuch. And it must have been this doctrine which St. Paul received from the Christian Church: "I delivered unto you that which I also received, how that Christ died for our sins according to the scriptures; and that he was buried, and that he rose again the third day according to the scriptures"; for the words "according to the scriptures" are sufficient to fix the reference to Isaiah liii. In only one passage[1] of his extant epistles does St. Paul make direct reference to this prophecy, but its teaching underlies not a few passages. It may explain 2 Cor. v. 21, which the older commentators translated "He who knew no sin was made *a sin offering* for us, that we might be made the righteousness of God in him." So in Rom. iii. 24 it is said that God set forth Christ Jesus as a propitiatory sacrifice, that we might be justified by His blood, accepted in faith; and this is repeated in v. 9, "We are now vouchsafed righteousness in virtue of his blood."

The absence of more distinct reference in St. Paul's Epistles to the prophecy of the suffering Servant of Jehovah is certainly remarkable.

---

[1] Rom iv. 25, "who was delivered for our offences."

It may be explained, and the paucity of sacrificial references may certainly be explained, by St. Paul's habit of getting down to the ideas that underlay the figures of the Old Testament, and especially the sacrificial symbols ; and the Western world, to which such imagery is strange, owes him a debt of gratitude for so doing. A Western mind may arrive by study at some comprehension of what St. Paul meant when he said, " Christ our passover is sacrificed for us " (1 Cor. v. 7) ; but how much more intelligible we find such a passage as the following, which expresses the same truth divested of its symbolic garb : " Have this mind in you, which was also in Christ Jesus ; who being in the form of God, counted it not a prize to be on an equality with God, but emptied himself, taking the form of a servant, being made in the likeness of men ; and being found in fashion as a man he humbled himself, becoming obedient even unto death, yea the death of the cross " (Phil. ii. 5, R.V.).

This language speaks straight home to us, and we can parallel it with words of our Lord Himself : " If any man would come after me, let him deny himself and take up his cross, and follow me " (Mark viii. 34). Similarly the assurance that follows, " Wherefore also God highly exalted him," coupled with the assurance that He who thus humbled Himself was by origin " in the form of God," conveys its meaning to the modern mind more simply than the phrase which St. Paul uses in another place, " whom God set forth to be a propitiation " (Rom. iii. 25). And, finally, the idea represented by the application of the sacrifice to those for whom it is offered, whether by keeping a feast upon the victim or being sprinkled with its blood, is for us more intelligibly and more cogently expressed in the direct statement, " By the obedience of the one the many are made righteous " (Rom. v. 19). This is, of course, the same doctrine as that of the prophet, who said of God's righteous Servant, " by whose stripes we are healed "; for it was not by His sufferings as sufferings that He brought healing, but by His sufferings in the cause of His obedience to the righteous law of God. St. Paul's two great words, " obedient unto death," and " by the obedience of the one the many are made righteous," sum up the teaching of that great ancient prophecy, although they do not quote its exact terms.

The question remains, *How* are the many made righteous by the obedience of the One ? It is to this question that St. Paul devotes much of his thought.

In the earlier epistles, which are concerned chiefly with practical matters of the Christian life, St. Paul is satisfied to refer to the doctrine of the Cross in general terms, as when he writes to the Thessalonians that Jesus Christ " died for us that we should live together with him " (1 Thess. v. 11), and to the Corinthians, that " God was in Christ reconciling the world unto himself, not reckoning unto them their trespasses " (2 Cor. v. 19). But already in this same passage of the letter to the Corinthians we have a sentence which shows that a theory of the Cross had shaped itself in St. Paul's mind. "We thus judge," he says, "that one died for all, therefore all died." Can we to-day put ourselves at the point of view from which St. Paul made this and similar judgments? To understand them we must recall once more the story of his conversion. There was in his own life a sharp line between his life under the law and his life under grace. He drew a line equally sharp between the life of our Lord on the earth and His life after the Resurrection. Then he identifies by faith both the present life of the believer with the risen Lord, and the death of the Lord with the past life of the believer.

It is impossible to understand St. Paul's teaching as to the application of Christ's Atonement to mankind, unless we recognise its psychological basis. The fact of experience upon which the apostle relies is the contrast between an old life subject to the solicitations of sin, and a new life freed from such solicitations and rejoicing "in hope of the glory of God." The old life he speaks of as the life "of the flesh" because the flesh is the seat of the desires which tempt to sin; the new life he calls the life "of the spirit" because it is the life in which man's spirit, through the reinforcement of the Spirit of Christ, has overcome "the mind of the flesh." The passage from the one life to the other was effected in St. Paul's own case by the conviction and acknowledgment that Jesus was alive, that He had been raised from the dead by the power of God, and that He was therefore proved to be, as the Church asserted, the Son of God

(Rom. i. 4), strong and willing to make men righteous. Accordingly he formulates the universal principle: "If thou shalt confess with thy mouth Jesus as Lord, and shalt believe in thy heart that God raised him from the dead, thou shalt be saved" (Rom. x. 9). The necessary condition, therefore, of salvation is the power of *faith*, by which a man "knows" or acknowledges Christ, and "subjects himself to him"; nay, "puts on" Christ (Gal. iii. 27), that is to say, appropriates and identifies himself with Him.

Now this identification with Christ, in which Christianity consists, St. Paul habitually regards as a double process, or rather as an action which has two sides.[1] It is an identification both with Christ's death, and with His risen life. The latter involves the former. "You died," he writes to the Colossians (iii. 3), "and your life is hid with Christ in God." And of himself he says, "I have been crucified with Christ, yet I live; yet no longer I, but Christ liveth in me" (Gal. ii. 20).

---

[1] St. Paul's antithetical way of writing is sometimes a puzzle to readers, who imagine that he intends to attribute the several elements in the process of salvation to different incidents in Christ's Passion; the fact being that both Christ's Passion and man's salvation are single and indivisible actions or processes. A remedy for the error will be found in collecting from St. Paul's various letters, or from the same letter, a few of these phrases for comparison. Thus in Rom. iv. 25 we are told that Christ "*rose* for our justification"; but in v. 9 it is said "we are justified *in his blood*." Again, in vi. 7, speaking of being "*crucified*" with Christ, St. Paul says, "he that is dead [to his sin] is freed from it"; but in viii. 10 this condition of being "dead to sin" is said to depend upon the presence of Christ "in us."

St. Paul sees a symbol of this double identification in the sacrament of baptism, which presents the appearance of a burial and a resurrection. "We were buried with him through baptism into death, that like as Christ was raised from the dead by the glory of the Father, so we also might walk in newness of life. For if we have become united with him by the likeness of his death, we shall be also by the likeness of his resurrection" (Rom. vi. 4).

St. Paul, although he must have known the story of our Lord's earthly life, makes but few references to it;[1] it is summed up for him in the great action of its close, by which "he died to sin once for all" and rose again "according to the Spirit of holiness." The important thing for a man was not to have known Christ after the flesh (2 Cor. v. 16) but to know His present regenerating power as "the Lord from heaven"; and to become "a new creature." And we feel, as we read St. Paul's description of the Christian life, in such a passage as the eighth chapter of Romans, that for him, at his conversion, there had been indeed "a death to sin once for all"; the

---

[1] There is an interesting passage in Rom. viii. 3, which, on the most probable interpretation, refers to the course of our Lord's life on earth, as setting the example and securing the possibility of a life of righteousness for men while still "in the flesh." Because, says St. Paul, the law was not sufficient to free the flesh from sin, God sent His own Son in flesh like our sinful flesh, in order to deal with sin [περὶ ἁμαρτίας, as A.V. and R.V. marg.]. The fact that Christ, althought empted, lived a sinless life was God's sentence upon "sin in the flesh." And so sin is sentenced in our flesh also who live not by its dictates but by the Spirit of Christ.

old things were entirely passed away. But to
many Christians to-day this complete separation
between the old and the new life remains an
ideal; and to them it is very comforting to find
that there were others like them in the first age.
For we find passages in St. Paul's epistles which,
with a fine sense of reality, break through the
figure, which baptism holds up, of a sudden and
complete death to the old nature, and a new
life of holiness perfect and entire ; and we have
instead the recognition that the one great fact
of Christianity is the gift of the Spirit of Christ,
by the power of which it is possible to subdue,
if not without effort, the old motives of the
flesh. "If Christ is in you, the body is dead :
if by the Spirit ye *mortify* the deeds of the body,
ye shall live" (Rom. viii. 10, 13). "Ye died, and
your life is hid with Christ in God: *mortify
therefore* your members which are upon the
earth" (Col. iii. 5). And the whole tone of the
appeal in the sixth chapter of Romans implies
that to some at least of those whom the apostle
was addressing the need for "mortifying" their
old nature was still a real experience. "We who
died to sin, how shall we any longer live therein ?
. . . Reckon ye yourselves to be dead unto
sin. . . . Let not sin reign in your mortal body,
that ye should obey the lusts thereof, neither
present your members unto sin as instruments of
unrighteousness." Even speaking of himself, the
apostle says with characteristic humility, " I count
all things but loss for the excellency of the
knowledge of Christ Jesus my Lord, . . . that I may
know him, and the power of his resurrection,

and the fellowship of his sufferings, *becoming* conformed unto his death [συμμορφιζόμενος], if by any means I may attain unto the resurrection of the dead" (Phil. iii. 8).

Perhaps some reference should be made, even in so slight a sketch, to a difficult text in Galatians (iii. 13) on which is sometimes based a theory of the Atonement which is essentially un-Pauline. The apostle says: "Christ hath redeemed us from the curse of the law, being made a curse for us: for it is written [Deut. xxi. 23], Cursed is every one that hangeth on a tree." This is sometimes explained to mean that Christ took our place, and suffered in our stead the curse of God which we had incurred by breaking the law. But the interpretation of the passage must be governed by that of a similar passage in chap. iv. 4: "When the fulness of the time was come, God sent forth his Son, made of a woman, made under the law, to redeem them that are under the law, that they might receive the adoption of sons." The expression "made a curse to redeem from a curse" is parallel to "made under the law to redeem from under the law"; and neither implies any doctrine of substitution. In the first passage, Christ is not said to have taken man's place under the curse, for the curses were different in the two cases; and in the second passage Christ is said to have put Himself under the law by the side of His people, not in their stead. In fact, both passages put in a very striking way the fundamental truth of the Incarnation, with its teaching as to Christ's perfect sympathy with His people. "In all their afflictions he was afflicted." He took man's nature upon Him, bearing their griefs and carrying their sorrows, submitting to all the limitations involved in race, and to all the consequences of ignorance and sin. It must be admitted that in both passages the language is rhetorical and cannot be construed literally; but the sense is clear. When, however, the attempt is made to interpret St. Paul's reference to the "curse" of the cross as a theological dogma, explaining it to mean that Christ took man's place under God's curse, which was the penalty of sin, it becomes necessary to point out that St. Paul here is for once speaking as a Jew to Jews, and not as a Christian to Christians. For when Christ said, " If any man will come after me, let him deny himself, and take up his cross and follow me," he abrogated the old Deuteronomic dogma as decisively as though He had said, in the Sermon on the Mount: "It was said to them of old time, Cursed is every one that hangeth on a tree, but I say unto you, Blessed are they that are crucified for righteousness' sake."

We must be on our guard, then, against forcing any single phrase of the great apostle out of harmony with his general teaching. His main doctrine is—and it lies upon the surface of his epistles, and he repeats it again and again— that the law of the spirit of life in Jesus Christ makes us free from the law of sin and death, and creates a new life in us, which is the life of an obedient son. Even though it be admitted that St. Paul gives a somewhat penal colouring in one or two passages to his expressions about our Lord's death, it is rather the colouring than the sense of what he says that differs from the teaching of the other apostolic writers and that of our Lord Himself. But we may feel sure that if we can say from our heart that we believe that God forgives us our sins for Christ's sake, or that He is "the Lamb of God who taketh away the sin of the world," or that "the Lord hath laid on him the iniquity of us all," St. Paul would say to us, as he said to the Corinthians, Who is Paul, or who is John, or who is Isaiah, but ministers through whom ye believed in Christ? The thing of importance is that Christ's Atonement should be preached and believed— not that any one theory of it, narrowed as all theories must be by individual limitations, should be accepted by the intelligence. It is worth noticing that in the few passages where St. Paul strikes a modern reader as Jewish and juridical, he never for an instant relaxes his hold on the great truth, that lies behind the Atonement, of the eternal love of God and His infinite willingness to forgive sin. St. Paul is at one with the whole prophetic teaching of the Scriptures in speaking not of God's reconciliation with men, but of man's reconciliation to God.[1] "God," he says, "was in Christ reconciling the world to himself" (2 Cor. v. 19). "God commendeth his

[1] Bp. Pearson, *On the Creed*, Art. X., calls this "the Socinian exception," and argues that the two phrases are identical in meaning. Our Second Article says, "Christ died to reconcile His Father to us." But it is wiser to stand by the language of Scripture. Bp. Pearson, if he had lived in this generation, would hardly have accused of Socianism Bps. Lightfoot and Westcott. See the former on Col. i. 21, and the latter on 1 John ii. 2.

own love towards us, in that while we were yet sinners Christ died for us" (Rom. v. 8). "God, being rich in mercy, for his great love wherewith he loved us, even when we were dead through our trespasses, quickened us together with Christ" (Eph. ii. 4). It is by God's grace that we are saved. The whole plan of redemption starts from God. There is no division of will between the Father and the Son, the one standing for justice, and the other for mercy. God Himself is declared to be both just and the justifier of him who believeth in Jesus.

If any man, then, is in Christ, joined to Christ by faith, he is a new creature, with new powers, used to a new issue. The life that he now lives by faith in the Son of God is life by the Spirit of God, its fruits the fruits of the Spirit. Conversely, if any man have not the Spirit of Christ —Christian though he calls himself—he is none of His. But to those who have the Spirit of Christ, their whole future life consists in a gradual assimilation to His likeness, from glory to glory: it may be an assimilation to His sufferings; for there are times when Christians may echo the words of the 44th Psalm, "We are killed all the day long,"—but no suffering can separate from the love of Christ, which is the love of God. Meanwhile, the word of exhortation for all of us is, "Put ye on the Lord Jesus Christ." As we say of Him, "In that he died, he died unto sin once; in that he liveth, he liveth unto God"; so may we reckon ourselves to be dead indeed unto sin, but alive unto God through Jesus Christ our Lord.

LECTURE VI

THE DOCTRINE OF THE EPISTLE TO THE HEBREWS

ATONEMENT in the Epistle to the Hebrews is represented as access to God, and the new life is life in God's presence. This access was made possible by our Lord's death on the cross, and how this could be is explained by the analogy of sacrifice. But that analogy is not quite what we might take it to be at first sight. Our Lord's work is not described metaphorically as a sacrifice: it is the only sacrifice; of it the Levitical sacrifices were but shadows. It is the reality; they are called sacrifices by metaphor from it, and the author gives the reason of this in chapter x., where he says that Christ's sacrifice took place in the sphere of the will. In the old sacrifices men represented the devotion of the will by means of unreasonable brutes; Christ came to do Himself the will of God. But how does this presentment of the doctrine affect us? Does it matter to us on which side the metaphor lies? Are not we, at any rate, using a metaphor when we speak of the Sacrifice of Christ? Perhaps we may see the answer to these questions more clearly if we first try to realise why the letter was written, to whom, and by whom.

The writer's name we do not know. We may be content to agree with Origen that he was not St. Paul, but one who knew the apostolic doctrine well.[1] And we find, in accordance with this judgment, that he does not so much add to the teaching of the other apostles, and especially of St. Paul, as put the same truths in another light, and (what is important to notice) he shows them in a particular application. His name we cannot tell, but we can read his character. He is a scholar, versed in Greek literature, with a delicate appreciation of the charm of language ; accustomed to philosophical discussion, yet more of an artist than a philosopher; using more of the technical language of philosophy than St. Paul, and yet in pure thought perhaps less deep. He thinks in pictures, and realises the unseen most readily in the sacramental mode. Things visible are to him effectual symbols of eternal truth, and the ancient ritual appears to him as a valuable symbol of the good things which were to come and now have come by Christ. The men he writes to are, like himself, Jews, with a pride in the history of their nation, scholars to whom his careful rhetoric is the fit language for the setting forth of the most solemn truth. He writes to them as to a little circle of intimate friends. He writes to them at a time of need, to encourage them to do one definite duty from which they shrink ; in an approaching crisis of faith he urges them to hold to the side of Christ. They had to face not merely danger, but a more subtle temptation, the conflicting claims

[1] Eusebius, *H. E.*, vi. 25.

of honour; loyalty to Christ might seem dis-
loyalty to another cause. We cannot be certain
about the explanation of all this, but the occasion
of the letter seems best represented in those
words of Dr. Hort's—" The day of the Lord
which the writer to the Hebrews saw drawing
nigh had already begun to break in blood and
fire when St. John sent his Apocalypse to the
Gentile Churches of Asia." [1] He refers to the
outbreak of the Jewish war with Rome. The
Jews had always chafed under the Roman yoke.
Their Messianic hope was, in the popular mind,
bound up with freedom from that foreign rule,
and the removal of all the poverty and wretched-
ness that was believed to be due to the present
state of things.[2] As time went on it became more
and more plain that the popular patriotic party
of the Jews would bring rebellion to a head and
fight for city and temple, liberty and religion.
These friends of the author's seem to have been,
as it were, the " philosophical liberals " of those
days. Their scholarly lives had not made the
, great ideas of liberty and patriotism less precious
to them, and the movement of the times comes
as an invitation. Now was the call to put
patriotism to the test, to awake from dreams,
to take action. Why not ? The Christians, it is
true, were on the other side. This was not the
way their Lord had marked out for the regenera-

---

[1] *Judaistic Christianity*, p. 160. But cf. Swete, *The Apocalypse
of St. John*, pp. xcviii-ci. Dr. Swete decides for the later date
for the Apocalypse, under Domitian.

[2] Cf. Shailer Mathews, *The Messianic Hope in the New
Testament*, Part I., ch. ii.

tion of society. They, though they might be
Jews, hung back, and bitter things were being
said about them, and bitter things would soon
be done by their fellow-countrymen. Why
should they hang back? Who was this Lord,
loyalty to whom required such a sacrifice? That
is another of their difficulties. The Epistle makes
it clear that they knew a great deal about Jesus
in "the days of his flesh." His noble character
had deeply impressed them. They regarded
Him with that kind of wonder which characterises
many of those to-day who are busy with the
records of the life of Jesus. They knew Him
human; they surmised something more; but
could they say, divine? To such men, in such
difficulties, their friend writes this letter. There
are three points in his treatment of them which
we must notice, for they will help us to understand the doctrine of the Epistle. First, he
writes to them as Jews; secondly, he means to
teach them who Christ is; thirdly, he means to
persuade them to keep on His side by a brave
exercise of will in the approaching crisis; and
he believes that their doing this last will clinch
for them what he has to say by way of argument.

They were Jews, and had been brought up in
the faith of Jews, which included the holding
of ancient ideas about sacrifice, deepened by
generations of divine training. The Epistle, it
is true, deals less with the Temple at Jerusalem
than with the Tabernacle of the Pentateuch, but
it is marked all through by a presupposition of
familiarity with the Jewish principle of sacrifice.
That principle is laid down in Lev. xvii. 11: "the

life of the flesh is in the blood : and I have given
it to you upon the altar to make atonement for
your souls : for it is the blood that maketh atonement by reason of the life." It may be that this
verse does not by itself carry us very far, but it
probably meant something quite plain and very
important to a Jew. So too the Epistle to the
Hebrews is not full enough in its explanation of
sacrifice to satisfy the Western mind, and this is
proved by the mistakes which have been made in
the application of its sacrificial language. That
language has been quoted again and again, but
it has nearly always been applied to something
different from sacrifice. St. Paul's thought of
" bought with a price " has governed the older
commentators' mind, and the blood, the offering,
the sacrifice, have been understood as a price
paid. Indeed, out of this there has arisen in
popular language a wrong use of the word
" sacrifice," and now, when anything is said to
be sacrificed, the chief idea presented is that of
loss. But in the Epistle to the Hebrews there is
nothing about a price paid ; and if sacrifice in the
writer's mind involves loss, it is that loss alone
of which our Saviour spoke when He said, " He
that loseth his life for my sake shall find it."
According to this Epistle the life which is
sacrificed is not lost or destroyed or impaired.
It passes through a change—perhaps always a
mysterious, dreadful change ; but it emerges free,
enriched, ready to be brought into the presence
of God. This is the doctrine which underlies
the saying in Leviticus that the life is in the
blood. This is the doctrine which rules the

whole of the Levitical ritual, where the sacrifice is by no means completed by the death of the victim, but by the transaction with the blood. That was sprinkled on the altar or on the worshipper, and in the great sacrifices of the Day of Atonement was carried by the high priest within the veil into the Holy of holies, and sprinkled upon the mercy-seat, where Jehovah had promised to meet His people. Here was the symbolism of the sacrifice, and it meant that a life not ended, but set free by death, was carried into the presence of God, and offered there to Him. The author of this Epistle takes for granted that his readers understand this principle of Jewish sacrifice.

We pass to the second characteristic of the first readers. They had need to learn who Jesus Christ is, and they had an imperfect grasp upon the doctrine of His Person. Neither they nor the writer appear to have seen Jesus Himself, but the memory of the " days of his flesh," as the author calls His visible life on earth, was vivid among them, and much of the beauty and power of the Epistle lies in the affectionate way in which His innocent, courageous, human life is pictured. This innocence, this unique freedom from sin, this unique and glorious victory in the utmost strain of temptation, is something which the author can take for granted that his friends admire as much as he does himself. He takes for granted, too, that they as thoroughly as himself are filled with wonder at His lordliness in the face of shame and danger, and at the wisdom and authority which made His teaching supreme. But it is also clear that these friends could not or would not explain the source of what they marvelled at. Once again, we find that they have inherited the mind of their nation. No one can read the Epistle and suppose for a moment that the cross of Christ, the suffering and death so heroically borne, were foolishness to them as to the Greeks; but they were a stumbling-block, and the author uses all his own faith and skill to remove this stumbling-block out of their way. Let us consider how he sets about this task. The Epistle opens with a great rolling sentence, where the very sound suggests a vast sea, of which the waves are the voices of the inspired teachers of all time past. He reminds them how all that broken sound has been gathered up in one voice at last, and he calls this last speaker Son of God (i. 2). He seems, as it were, to place his friends in heaven itself, and bids them from that vantage-point to contemplate God manifesting Himself in this Son, who is light visible streaming from the hidden glory, the character cut upon the seal to represent the idea which was hidden in the artist's mind (i. 3). Then he makes them see this light striking upon certain eminences in the history of the chosen people, this character impressing itself upon those Christs who were also called sons of God among men—now a king, and now the chosen people itself; and then, again, he points to the same light visible, the same Divine character, shining unchangeable through, and impressing itself upon, the varieties of all created things (i. 5-12). And then, without as yet affirming, he

13

suggests the question, "Is not this he whom you call your Lord?" (ii. 3). After this he sets them on earth again, and reminds them how a psalmist called God to witness that He had crowned man with glory and honour, setting him over the works of His hands, and putting all things in subjection under his feet. But, says our author, we do not yet see men in such honour; Jesus, however, we do behold, thus crowned with glory and honour for the suffering of death (ii. 5-9). Once more he has deepened their thought about their Lord, and by the introduction of those words "suffering" and "death" has prepared the way for an argument that he will presently develope at length. Besides that he has brought together the two aspects of this Lord's Person—the human and the divine— and he will proceed to show how One thus human and divine may really be believed to have visited His people.

But already this thought of "human and divine" enables him to introduce the word which will be most useful to him—namely High Priest (ii. 17). Jesus, the Son of God, laying hold on the one hand of the seed of Abraham, and on the other coming from God Himself, is the High Priest of men, standing on their Godward side, fit to make atonement for His people, and to lead them into the presence of God. The whole argument we cannot pursue now. This thought, however, of the High Priest is the one which served him best of all, and round it all he has to say is gathered. So after a page or two, we find him taking up the word again and pro-

ceeding to define the high-priestly work which
the Son of God has done. First he speaks of
the priesthood as they themselves have known
it, v. 1-3. And here it will be felt that he is not
simply referring to a priesthood represented in
a book. There is affection in his words towards
good priests whom he has known, priests able to
bear sympathetically with those who are ignorant
and out of the way, and who tried to do more
for them than merely to go through ceremonial
services. Indeed, much of the pathos of the Epistle
lies in this ; the priest of the Levitical course, with
all his splendid ritual, which it was hard enough
to see passing away, could never do the one
thing on which his heart was set, could never
cleanse the conscience of his people from dead
works to serve the living God. Therefore this
ancient ritual, so magnificent but so ineffectual,
was drawing near to vanishing away ; and rightly
so, for it was a mere ritual, a thing of shadows,
chiefly valuable as pointing to a reality which
existed all the time. Which existed all the time,
for long before the Levitical priesthood came
into being there had been indications even upon
earth of another Priesthood, eternal, real, be-
longing to the Son of God, whose priestly power
lay, not in the representative blood of bulls and
goats, however vividly that blood might symbolise
human or divine life, but in His own indissoluble
life. One such indication was found in the very
ancient history of Melchizedek, the priest of God
Most High, whose person was described by the
historian with such a mysterious reverence as made
it, so to say, an outline sketch of the ever-living

Son of God Himself (vii. 1-3). Another was afterwards given in the words of the psalmist who claimed the same royal priesthood for a king in Israel, once again setting forth in outline the picture of One greater than any earthly king (v. 6). And now the outlines have been filled up, resuming "the wonted substance to such their umbrated forme," and in the very suffering of Jesus the Lord the evidence of that eternal life is found manifested in sacerdotal offering, which belongs to priesthood after the order of Melchizedek (v. 10).

One thing which had to be filled up in the outline sketch was the victim. None is mentioned in connexion with Melchizedek or the psalmist's kingly Priest. In the Epistle this is filled up. The true Priest is His own Victim. Through His own blood Christ entered the heavenly sanctuary (ix. 12). So at once His suffering and death are accounted for. He suffered as men suffer, that He might have the true priest's fellowship and sympathy with His people. But more than that, the suffering was the preparation for the perfect obedience by which He did His work. He learned obedience by suffering (v. 8); in His humiliation and suffering He gained the crowning with glory and honour which was the signal of His determination to die (ii. 9); and the whole course of suffering was finished in the mysterious act of death which was the outward and visible sign only. As the blood of bull or goat symbolised the life with which the Levitical priest entered the sanctuary and made his offering, so the blood visibly shed on

Calvary signified that at the moment of finishing "the days of the flesh," Jesus, now Christ and High Priest indeed, entered the very presence of His Father "through his own blood," that is, in His own indissoluble life (vii. 16); that was the offering with which He entered, and in virtue of which He remains in the real sanctuary, the very presence of God.

And here, before we go on to consider how this offering can be considered to affect mankind, let us pause a moment to ask what the Epistle represents Him as doing still in the heavenly sanctuary. It might seem that the author answers this question definitely enough. Taking up some words of St. Paul, he says that " He ever liveth to make intercession for " us (vii. 25 ; cf. Rom. viii. 34). But these words do not quite solve the difficulty. Intercession may be said to include prayer, but it means more than that. Does it mean "offering"? Is that sacrifice being still offered though not repeated? The Epistle emphatically denies that it can be repeated ; but why? May we say "Because it is an eternal sacrifice"? Now, even if it be granted that "eternal," as used by the author, can be applied to succession in time, it must however be noticed that, often as he uses the word "eternal," he never applies it to the sacrifice itself, and at the end of chapter ix. he rather significantly introduces another word instead of "offer" or "sacrifice": "Christ," he says, "did not enter into a sanctuary made with hands but into heaven itself, now to appear before the face of God for us" (ix. 24). It seems as though he felt that the language of sacrifice did not after all carry him far enough in treating of these vast realities, and that for a worthy presentment of the enduring activity of Christ, and His continued connexion with the struggling, yearning race of men, a simpler picture were needed, a picture less defined by sharp lines. It is the appearing, the presence of Christ, the simply being before God, that sums up His abiding activity on our behalf—" by this prevailing Presence we appeal." Thus the death on Calvary will be the outward sign; the offering of His life set free, the invisible act of Christ's sacrifice. That sacrifice, offered once for all, inaugurated His new state of activity for men; but though indeed that state continues, it should not be called a continuing sacrifice, but rather unceasing action, and at the same time perfect rest—for He is now "apart from sin "—on the basis of the inaugurating sacrifice. His attitude towards the Father is not now that of sacrificing, offering; His life and all that He inherits He has offered once for all; now, on the basis of that one offering, He is present with the Father in Royal Priesthood. " He sat down at the right hand of God; from henceforth expecting, till his enemies be made the footstool of his feet. For by one offering he hath perfected for ever them that are sanctified " (x. 12-14).

That seems the answer to the question which best satisfies all the passages which might be quoted from the Epistle. Now we go on to the further question. Supposing the death of Christ to have issued in this priestly offering, is there

any connexion between that offering of His own
life on the one hand and the lives of men on the
other hand, which can be not merely suggested
by analogy, but certainly established? We are
to consider, that is to say, how the author
represents this work of Christ as affecting men.
And in doing so we shall be led insensibly to
that third point in his treatment of his friends—
his appeal to them to keep faithful to the side
of Christ. He did indeed prepare us for accepting such an effect in chapter ii., when he
said that "both he that sanctifieth and they
that are sanctified are all of one" (ii. 11). That,
however, was one of his preparatory notes. He
generally prepares beforehand by some such
note for each argument, but he never forgets
to elaborate the argument in due time. In
this case he has three main lines of reasoning
—the Covenant, the Opened Way, the Power
of Will.

A covenant, he says, is always based on a
sacrificial death, and the death of Christ, with
its more than symbolical blood-shedding, inaugurated that New Covenant which Jeremiah
promised (ix. 15-17, viii. 8-12), and which our
Lord Himself claimed to be bringing in when
at the Last Supper He said, "This is my blood
of the covenant," or "of the new covenant."
Those who have been sprinkled with that blood,
and the Epistle seems to imply that all who have
been baptized have been thus sprinkled (x. 22),
are under the New Covenant, and in a new
relationship with God, through the blood of
Christ its Mediator. Perhaps this appears to

us hardly an argument, but only another analogy which rouses thought yet proves nothing. The objection may be justified, yet it should be remembered that all through the Epistle an appeal to the heart mingles with argument, and if it really was written to Jews just when the fate of Jerusalem seemed hanging in the balance, and the ancient glories of the nation nigh to vanishing away, in that time of reformation when the Roman army was on the march, the full quotation in chapter viii. of Jeremiah's words, first spoken when Jerusalem was invested by the Chaldean armies, would strike a blow upon the heart of the readers. And if it was little more than thirty years ago that the Lord had spoken those other words and then straightway laid down His life for His friends, that reminiscence too would have a strange influence :

She sigh'd,
The infant Church ! Of love she felt the tide
Stream on her from her Lord's yet recent grave.[1]

To pass, however, to the second line of argument. Our Lord, says the Epistle, has entered by His death within the veil ; " having therefore, brethren, boldness to go the way into the holy place in the blood of Jesus, the way which he inaugurated for us, a way fresh slain yet living through the veil, that is the way of his flesh. . . . Let us draw near " (x. 19-22).[2] He has gone before ; He has opened the way, and now we may go along it. Yet there must be

[1] M. Arnold, *The Good Shepherd with the Kid.*
[2] Cf. Westcott *ad loc.*

no mistake what the way is. It is the way of
Jesus' flesh, a way of courage, patience, obedience, suffering, humiliation—a way where life
is found in death. If the argument of the
Covenant might to a sensitive heart pass into
an appeal, how necessarily this does! With what
especial necessity to those first readers, who had
their plain, hard duty before them, and were,
as their friend supposed, outside the Sabbath of
the people of God, and the heavenly sanctuary
cleansed and enlightened by Christ's offering,
until they followed His example, and went after
Him the way fresh slain yet living of His
flesh.

And so we, with them, are brought quite
naturally to the third line of argument. The
reality of Christ's sacrifice lay above all, says
the writer, in its being offered in the sphere of
Will, or, as he magnificently phrases it in one
place, "through eternal spirit" (ix. 14). The
Levitical sacrifices offered brute victims, and no
real exercise of will took place. When Jesus
came it was as though He were heard uttering
the psalmist's words, "Lo, I am come to do
thy will, O God." When He offered Himself,
having learnt obedience by suffering, He offered
His will to God, and lost it, to find it perfected
in union with God's will : " By which will we have
been sanctified through the offering of the body
of Jesus Christ once for all " (x. 5-10). Is there
really need to ask how that offering of the body
of Jesus Christ could effect this ? Does not every
one who has a duty before him from which he
shrinks know the answer ? Would not those

14

friends of the writer's know it who had in an earlier time of trial learnt the value of the possession of their true selves, lost and found in willing sacrifice, and who were now reading his letter just when patriotism, ancient ties, and apostasy were offered to them on the one side, and on the other the example of the Lord, who had set His face so decidedly against this false revolutionary dream of Christship, whom they remembered with such affection, who (as their friend knew well) would shine out clearly to them as the only Christ, the effectual Saviour, if they followed Him ?

Follow Him, your Forerunner. That exhortation sounds all through the letter. St. Paul's great thought " in Christ " is never expressed, though it may not necessarily have been absent from the writer's mind. He puts things more pictorially than St. Paul, and might perhaps have found some other way of presenting the same truth. But what holds his pen is the indecision of his friends. They are not yet practically " in Christ," and he (knowing them well) knows that to say with St. Paul " You already live in Christ, and therefore will do this thing," will not result in their obedience. He rather says, " Your Lord has gone before you, having through courage and suffering offered the sacrifice on your behalf. By that sacrifice there has been remission of past sin. You are free from sin as He was, but as He was you are strained by temptation. Follow Him and you will know that sacrifice to be effectual." And so, having concluded in chapter x. the properly argumentative part of his letter, he calls on them for faith to be courageous. Of thought and argument these scholars have often had their fill. The heroes of their nation, who by their faith did their duty so bravely, are waiting to bear witness to the effect of faith in them (xi.—xii. 1). This leads to one of a series of three illustrations by which the author punctuates his letter, urging more and more closely the connexion between faith in the Master who has entered heaven and courageous action on the part of His servants. The first is in chapter vi., where the servants are likened to the crew of a ship which has finished its voyage and lies outside the harbour. The anchor has been dropped into the mysterious deep, and holds the ground. The captain has already gone ashore, and the crew are waiting for the signal to follow him. The second is in chapter xii., following the passage on faith. Here the servants are like athletes, standing in the arena, with the contest about to begin. They are at that trying point when the athlete strips off his clothing—unwillingly, it so easily besets him—and has to shiver with excitement for a moment before the word is given to start. But now they may see their Lord seated in His heavenly place at the end of the course. If they will run, faith passes into clear sight. The last is in chapter xiii.; and here, if it is an illustration, it is something more. It is rather a sacrament than a picture that is set forth. The bodies of the victims in sin offerings used to be burnt outside the camp. So Jesus suffered. The death on Calvary seemed, as far as men could see, to be less a sacrifice than the offscouring of a sacrifice. And yet when Jesus died like that before the eyes of men, He entered—though men could not see this—as the immortal, glorious Priest into the presence of His Father. Would any understand such symbolism, trust such an effect of death, realise that He does live still, and enter that peace and glory with Him? That can only be by going His way, by seeking Him without the camp, by losing life, by breaking will, to find it—in a word, by offering sacrifice.

Argument has passed into appeal. Appeal leads on to prayer. The letter ends with a prayer—symmetrical, terse, pregnant with theology, the very type of our Western collects (xiii. 20, 21). In the later text the special application was lost—perhaps that the verses might be better fitted for general reading. In the Revised Version the original form has been restored, and we see the writer on his knees, a true sharer in the Priesthood of Christ; for his own will has been lost and found, and all he needs to ask for himself is that the God of Peace (still making peace in troubled hearts and dangerous times) may "continue to work in us that which is well pleasing in his sight." But for his friends he makes request for the one boon he has had at heart all the while he has been arguing and pleading: "may the God of peace make you perfect in every good thing to do this one act of his will." To these two petitions two aspects of the Lord's work correspond. Jesus, the great human Shepherd, our Lord, went to, and in the

blood of the eternal Covenant was brought again
from the dead—there is the way He may be
followed; and the whole prayer is offered
through Jesus Christ, to whom belongs the
divine, immortal glory, which is the Sabbath
rest of all who have followed Him and entered
the sanctuary of God. The prayer teaches us
how to read the Epistle. In this Epistle, as in
the rest of Holy Scripture, Atonement means
man's reconciliation to God and union with
God in Christ. The special circumstances of the
readers have caused the doctrine to be set forth
in a special manner. Hence certain omissions,
as they might seem if we took the letter to be
a theological treatise. We are not told how the
one remission is to be applied to the daily sins
of Christ's people, who nevertheless are infirm
and do sin daily; the writer has one special
sin in view, and means to save his friends from
committing it. Except for two or three brief
allusions, the solemn sacrifice of daily worship
and daily life is not brought into connexion with
the liturgical offering of Christ; the writer's
whole attention is concentrated on one special
act of sacrifice which at that very time his friends
must make. But besides these omissions there
is a point on which we might, if we were careless,
misunderstand him. He lays so much stress on
the act of will the readers are to make, that we
might suspect him of teaching that Atonement
begins with man's effort, not with God's gift.
The prayer directs us to read the whole
Epistle more truly, recognising that whether
striving to follow, or peace in having followed,

be the immediate lot of any man, each has been made possible for him only by the living way which Jesus Christ, doing the Father's will, has inaugurated—" such a high priest became us."

Printed by Hazell, Watson & Viney, Ld., London and Aylesbury, England.